SCOTT

STUD, ...

CEMETERIES. I'LL SEE YOU THERE...

Joe Teeples

Ghostology 101

A Ghost Hunters Guide
by
Ross Allison and Joe Teeples

authorHOUSE

1663 LIBERTY DRIVE, SUITE 200
BLOOMINGTON, INDIANA 47403
(800) 839-8640
www.authorhouse.com

First published by AuthorHouse 10/04/05

ISBN: 1-4208-8121-3 (sc)

Library of Congress Control Number: 2005908885

Printed in the United States of America
Bloomington, Indiana

This book is printed on acid-free paper.

Ghostology 101 – A Ghost Hunters Guide
Ross Allison/Joe Teeples

Table of Contents

The Stories

People love to be frightened. That is the principle behind amusement parks, horror books and spooky movies. The authors of ghost stories and movie producers who specialize in this type of fare would have us believe that a typical haunting would go like this…

It was a dark and stormy night. Cold rain fell incessantly on the Victorian mansion as lightning tore through the sky. The flash illuminated the family graveyard behind the aging wooden structure that had been empty since the last of the Bastion family had died off in a mysterious accident only weeks after writing to their pastor that "The house is out to get me."

Pastor McMean pushed his way past the overgrown bushes as he approached the front door. Was there a movement inside the house, or was that just his imagination? As he reached for the door knob the floorboards beneath him groaned and the door knob itself jiggled a bit. He grasped the door knob, pushed the door open on its squeaky hinges and entered the dark hallway. Turning on

his flashlight he saw a light down the hall and a mysterious figure, then the door creaked shut behind him.

He felt as if he was being watched as he turned and headed towards the staircase. The sound of footsteps could be heard coming down the staircase as the Pastor froze in place.

He whirled just in time to see the door close and when he turned around to confront the figure, he saw nothing but shadows. He pointed his flashlight at the empty staircase in time to see a whirling mist solidify before his very eyes and take on the form of an old man with a patch over one eye. The apparition's lips were moving, and McMean could faintly hear words that became clearer with each passing moment, "Get out of my house....."

The dedicated ghost hunter would give anything to find a ghost haunt that could be documented as firmly as that scenario would be. Unfortunately; investigation often provides rational explanations for the events described by Pastor McMean. He would be taken more seriously if he had been accompanied by someone who would testify to the accounts of the evening.

With a storm outside and wind buffeting the house, it would be normal for strange sounds to come from the walls as water ran down the gutters, eaves and walls and animals sought shelter from the storm in the now deserted house. Lights could be attributed to lighting flashes or cars on the roadway and the mysterious figure that disappeared into the shadows could simply have been the pastors' reflection in a mirror.

The whirling ectoplasm could be dust that was disturbed by the visitor to the house and the ghostly apparition with the demand to be left alone could be accounted for by the fact that Pastor McMean had been reading a Steven King novel recently.

All of these events could have a rational explanation.... Or could they? It is the job of the ghost hunter to explain routine events and to find and investigate the true anomalies.

Along the way ghost hunters discover a land rich with historical side notes. Unlike history courses in schools that may be based on dates and calendars, these investigators discover the people and events that made our land great. When researching cemeteries and ghosts they discover the people behind the plaque on the wall. While the plaque may reveal that an historical event took place, ghost hunters discover the people behind those events in all their human glory and frailty.

REGISTERED
TOMBSTONE HISTORIC DISTRICT
ON THIS SITE

THE LONGHORN RESTAURANT

ONCE THE OWL CAFE BEFORE THAT THE BUCKET OF BLOOD WHERE VIRGIL EARP WAS SHOT FROM THE SECOND STORY WINDOW.

The Ghost Hunters

Many organizations study ghosts and the largest is probably the International Ghost Hunting Society. Most serious ghost hunting organizations refer to and rely on the IGHS for guidance, assistance and a network to share information. People who hunt ghosts come from all walks of life and share a common interest in ghosts and ghostly activity.

In northwest Washington state the Amateur Ghost Hunters Of Seattle Tacoma (A.G.H.O.S.T.) is the most active ghost hunting group in the state. This voluntary organization has open membership meetings which are held twice a month in Federal Way, Washington. They also provide classes and a venue for people to share their ghost hunting experiences. AGHOST members participate in group activities such as ghost hunts, expeditions, and investigations and share their experiences with others. They also gather for fun activities such as ghost related movies, theater and other events. They've even gone bowling together.

The organization seeks serious and open-minded people who would want to volunteer and help form an investigation team in the northwest area. Meetings are held every other Sunday. Some investigations could involve over night stays in haunted places and other activities. Individuals who want to learn about the spirit world around us and the curious are also welcome to attend the open meetings. Members are required to attend one meeting a month in order to be considered for participation in onsite investigations.

To become a member interested parties should attend a new members meeting, where they will be introduced to the organization and how it functions. After joining the organization, members receive their Ghost Hunters Handbook, name tag and membership card. In order to participate in ghost investigation members must be trained as an observer, a technician or a psychic. These training sessions are available to members only and are provided at no charge.

Official club apparel is available and members are encouraged to wear their T shirts or name tags at meetings and organization functions to identify them as members of the group. AGHOST conducts an average of three to four investigations a month, averaging 30-40 investigations a year. A database of their investigation summaries, technical reports, photographs, Electronic Voice Phenomenon (EVP), and video clips has been compiled and is continuously updated.

Members get to join other like minded souls on a quest for ghosts and haunted events in their area. Some of these hunts include overnight investigations with all the equipment and others are simply excursions to cemeteries or other historical areas to gather information. In any event, members get plenty of time to practice their skills, and even lay around in cemeteries before their time has come, as evidenced by the photo of one of our members here, getting a shot of a tombstone.

The Theories of Life After Death

Human society evolved from a hunter-gatherer group to family units to a society that was able to feed itself and grow into social organizations. As it did the society began to ponder more lofty thoughts such as different forms of government and technology for building, manufacturing and farming. Other thoughts began to develop regarding the afterlife. Cultures tend to vary in their beliefs about the afterlife and these differences are reflected in the way that they respond to the death of their members.

Early Hebrew scripture mentions the living attempting to contact the dead. The ancient Egyptians created a guide to what they considered the final destination for souls. This "book of the dead" described the judgment and rebirth of an individual. They felt that the soul had two parts, one which carried the personality of the individual, those characteristic traits that make each human unique and another part that was the life force of the entity.

Ancient Egyptians believed that when they died the soul would split into several parts and continue to live in an afterlife. These parts were spirit forms called the ba, the akh, and the ka. The ba was the individuals' personality and is often depicted as a bird with a human head. Thos who lived worthy lives would spend eternity in the "fields of Yam" which was believed to be a land of peace and plenty. Later generations of Egyptians felt that only the most deserving would have this peace by joining Osiris in the underworld. Nobles were often buried with the Egyptian Book of the Dead which would serve as a guidebook for their transition to the afterlife.

The ka was the person's life force or soul and resembled the person; at the instant of death it was felt that this flew to the start to spend eternity in the heavens. The akh is usually depicted by the crested ibis bird. Since the ka resembled the person it would have to use artifacts that the person was familiar with during life, hence the items found in tombs. Since the ka needed a form to inhabit, the body must be preserved to ensure eternal life.

Mummification took about 70 days to complete. Several embalmers worked on the body under the guidance of a chief priest who wore a mask representing Anubis, the god of mummification. The body had to be rid of any soft body parts that would cause decay, so an

incision was made on the left side of the abdomen to remove the organs. The removed organs were preserved in a special mixture of table salt and baking soda then placed in canopic jars.

The brain was also removed by breaking the bone that separates the nasal cavity from the brain using a sharp instrument and inserting it in the nose. Then a long hook would be used to stir up the brain and liquefy it. The body would be turned face down to allow the brain to seep out the nostrils. The Egyptians felt that the only purpose of the brain was to product snot! The body would then be washed and rubbed with spices. Wine was used to wash the body and the alcohol in the wine served as an antiseptic and killed bacteria. Then the body could be adorned with jewelry, covered in linen strips and magical amulets to protect the mummy so that the ka could live forever.

The Greeks honored their dead by inviting the spirits into their homes for a feast. This ritual recognized the concept of life after death and the idea that spirits continued in an afterlife with a will. By showing respect at the feast the Greeks felt that the spirits would be content to remain in the next world and not haunt them.

The Roman's felt that spirits acted as guardian angels, but also believed in evil spirits. They held a three day festival to make the spirits happy so that they would leave the living alone. The Chinese honored their ancestors by conducting rituals, as did the Hindu who had a celebration that lasted for ten days. This belief in an afterlife is an important part of every culture.

The Day of the Dead has been celebrated in Mexico for centuries and is a celebration based on a mixture of Aztec and Catholic beliefs to recognize those who have passed on. Mexicans traditionally believe that if the dead are uncared for or ignored they may take revenge on the living. October 31 is All Hallows Eve and the spirits of dead children are invited back to the homes. On November 1, All Saints Day, the family honors their ancestors by inviting the adult spirits to visit. Candles are lit and placed along the street as luminaries to guide the spirits home. November 2 is All Souls Day when people attend church and visit the cemetery afterwards to decorate the graves of their loved ones. Families would often have a picnic on the family grave site in remembrance of the departed relative. In earlier times they would dig up the skull of their family members for this event.

The age of spiritualism was ushered in when three sisters claimed to be able to communicate with the dead in 1847. The Fox sisters claimed that a series of rapping noises was communication with a peddler who had been murdered and was buried beneath their house. A skeleton was found in the basement and seemed to confirm the demise of the peddler and the girls became celebrities. They developed and demonstrated their ability to communicate with sprits using taps and knocks, automatic writing and even voices as the spirit took control of the girls. Other mediums got on the band wagon and soon séances were being conducted around the nation in semi-dark rooms where cold breezes would blow, tables would tilt and fresh flowers would materialize out of thin air. Belief in the ability to communicate with those who have passed on rapidly grew and became an organized religion called Spiritualism. Even after Magaretta Fox demonstrated in 1888 how she had fraudulently produced the spirit rapping, dedicated spiritualists did not believe her recantation. Even Sir Arthur Conan Doyle did not believe her confession. Shortly before her death in 1895, Margaretta recanted her confession in a written statement.

The Baganda of Uganda believes that the soul turns into an invisible ghost that retains many characteristics of the dead person. This ghost remains with the family, and if it is not pleased it can bring illness and death. The Baganda'n belief is that two years after a death the ghost will enter the body of a newborn infant in the same family.

During the 19th century it became common for people to seek a medium or psychic to attempt to communicate with the dead. One method of communication was a stylus that participants would lightly lay their fingers on as it rested on a board with letters and symbols that would spell out the message from beyond. This method of communication became much more popular after the toy manufacturers, Parker Brothers, redesigned the board and marketed the device as a parlor game.

Thomas Edison (1847-1931) believed that that the soul was made up of what he referred to as "life units." It was felt that these microscopic particles could rearrange themselves into any form and retained the full memory and personality of the person. These life units were considered to be indestructible. Edison was working on a secret project at the end of his life to create a machine that would let the living see and communicate with the souls of the dead. Edison's machine was designed to detect life units in the environment and allow living individuals to communicate with the dead.

What is paranormal activity?

The term paranormal means "beyond-normal". "Normal" is a very subjective term. Normalcy to a blind person is significantly different from that of a person who has the gift of sight. Within the visual world of those who can see, color blind people have another view of normal. For our purposes, normal is defined as phenomena that can be explained by known physical laws of nature.

Ghosts have been talked about since the beginning of time and are commonly defined as a disembodied soul. The soul of a dead person is commonly believed to inhabit an unseen world and that it may appear to the living in bodily likeness. This disembodied soul may have missed its chance to move on to a higher plane, or sometimes didn't realize that it has passed away. Sometimes ghosts seem to be oblivious to the fact that they are being observed and perform the same actions over and over again while other ghosts recognize that they are being viewed and tolerate viewing with no interaction with the living. Other ghosts seem to possess intellectual skills and a desire to communicate with the living. Some investigators use the term "ghost" to describe those anomalies that do not seem to possess will or intellect. They would consider a haunting where the same person is seen walking across the room as if it were the 1800's as a ghost. If the specter stops and interacts with the investigator that would indicate intellect and a free will. If the specter attempts to communicate, this would be considered a spirit.

Some investigators feel that a ghost is an entity that refuses or is unable to go to the "Other Side". These entities stay in a location that feels comfortable, even if the surroundings and people have changed. These entities exhibit behavior and personalities as if they were still alive and continue to do what they used to do as if nothing has changed.

Ghosts may realize that something is different, but they do not realize that they have passed on. This makes them confused and sometimes angry. Ghosts can be possessive of physical and material things, whether these items belong to them or not. Anything that will offer a small comfort to them in their confused state is coveted and sometimes even removed.

A "Residual Haunting" is technically not being caused by ghosts. It is one of those time/space/continuum types of things, where the sounds and visuals of a historical moment are being transported into this time period. You can tell a residual haunting, as the "ghosts" do not acknowledge anyone's presence but their own. Examples of Residual haunting Sites include Civil War Battle Sites, murder scenes and places that hold extremely high-energy.

Like a photograph, a residual haunting is saved in time and space by highly-charged emotional distress. This image will playback itself time and time again. This is what a lot of "ghost voices". These repeat the same thing over and over that might be recorded as EVP may be. The tape recorder is actually picking up voices from the experiences and circumstances of distressing events. These types of events leave behind a "footprint" in time. In turn, they can then become "residuals".

It is interesting to note that where residuals sightings take place it is not uncommon for investigators to discover more than one ghost, sometimes from vastly different eras.

Some ghost hunters regard a spirit to be an intelligent entity that may travel from the "Other Side" to ours on a regular basis. These spirits may be attracted to certain people, places and things or they may be simply visiting our plane of existence. They return to the "Other Side" when their visit is complete. They seem to be conscious and are aware that they have passed on.

Female ghosts often tend to feel sadder and emotionally distraught. There is more empathy associated with a female spirit and their reason for not moving on may be based on severe emotional distress. Female ghosts may appoint themselves the caretaker of a building, library, child, or family situation. Male ghosts tend to be more aggressive and may be irritable and/or possessive. They may break, move or steal objects, or do things in an attempt to deliberately annoy or frighten the investigator.

The "Confused Dead" constitute a minority of hauntings. These ghosts are often the victims of a violent death, have committed suicide or died while unconscious or suffered from insanity. They may not be aware that they have passed over. Infrequently, these spirits are so wrapped up within their own infinite purgatory that they do not recognize other ghosts or the living. These confused entities still believe that they are alive, and wander aimlessly awaiting a fate that has already transpired. These spirits are very hard to communicate with. They are bound in this state for all eternity and are not conscious enough to realize what is going on around them.

The "Conscious Dead" constitutes the majority of ghosts and hauntings. These people are aware that something is different. They refuse to leave a residence or a place where they feel comfortable. These ghosts could have met a violent or unnatural demise and may be aware that they are dead but have chosen to stay in this dimension. Many times, entities are awaiting some type of validation or unfinished business before they decide to move on. At other times they have chosen to be where they are and are not interesting in leaving. There may be more than one of them in one location in many cases, and in many cases they know about one another, but do not socialize. Investigators may be able to carry on a conversation with this type of spirit.

The "Guardian Spirit" or "Visitors" are persons who have passed on, but visit loved ones time and again. These spirits are usually described as a "comfortable" or "helpful" presence. Sometimes they are family members, other times they have just chosen to stay in a home or a location where they have appointed themselves guardian.

These visitors show up at family reunions, marriages, births, deaths, or other important and life changing matters, offering guidance to facilitate a goal that is trying to be reached by the living, receiving party. In most of these cases the spirit(s) will not stay, but are passing through as they help the living reach the common goal and to let them know that "they are alright." Many of the orbs that show up on film may be "visitors".

Ghost hunters may encounter a variety of evidence of an apparition, such as:

- Shadows
- Sounds
- Ectoplasm
- Ghosts
- Spirits
- Full Phantoms

Apparitions

The rough definition of an apparition is the manifestation of the soul or thinking entity of a deceased person, animal or sentient being. They are also referred to as a ghost or spirit and are seen visually. This is what every ghost hunter seeks, to see the ghost chasing him or her down the hall as evidence of the supernatural. Apparitions are very seldom alike, varying in size, shape, image and conduct of movement.

Ghost hunters try to group apparitions into categories for ease of cataloguing. This makes it easier to discuss and compare notes between different cases and types of hauntings.

The atmospheric apparition is thought to be an imprint of energy that remains from a past event. These events could be tragic or violent and the energy imprint causes some witnesses to report seeing a replay of events as they happened in the past. Some images are visual while some have sound and scent. An example could be the civil war soldier who walks along a stretch of battleground night after night. Sometimes witnesses report hearing murmurs or whispers and even smelling tobacco smoke, although no one in their party is smoking at the time. Atmospheric apparitions tend to fade over time as the image and sounds become more and more faint.

One theory on apparitions has been demonstrated using quantum physics as light particles become suspended in the atmosphere and remain dormant until some outside variable stimulates the particles. As they become stimulated they vibrate and it is thought that witnesses see the frozen light particles vibrating which creates a vision of the past event. The conditions for this to take place would be indoors in areas where weather cannot interfere with the demonstration. The apparitions may only be visible from a certain distance or angle, so that only a small portion of the ghost hunting group may be able to view the apparition.

Historical apparitions haunt older homes and tend to appear in solid forms. They are usually dressed in period clothing and do not communicate with the ghost hunters or even acknowledge the presence of the witnesses. They may be seen in more than one area of the facility or residence.

Recurring apparitions occur in a cyclic pattern over a period of time, such as the annual anniversary of an event. This is one of the most popular types of sightings and can include ghosts of people and animals. Recurring  apparitions may appear on the anniversary of the date that they committed suicide, were murdered or, in the case of soldiers, marching across battlefields on the anniversary of a great battle.

Not all ghosts died hundreds of years ago. There is a fresh crop every day and some have the look, feel and even smell of modern day people. These are called modern apparitions and may look dated as time passes, but at present they look just like normal people.

The crisis apparition occurs shortly after people die. When people are on their death bed it is not uncommon for ghost sightings to occur as the ghost attempts one last time to say a final goodbye, fulfill a promise or express love to ease the sadness of the living. This type of ghost rarely hangs around for more than a few days to accomplish their task, and then moves on.

Family apparitions seem to become attached to a particular family and haunt members of the family, even through successive generations. These ghosts may include the spirits of deceased family members and even of their animals. It is reported that some of these ghosts may be a harbinger of death, signaling that someone in the family is about to die.

Haunted objects may be referred to as object apparitions or cursed objects. While most hauntings seem to be centered around some type of a ghost this instance occurs when a particular object seems to be the center of ghostly activity. Some objects held a strong emotional tie to a person while other objects leave no clue as to why they seem cursed. Strange occurrences such as sound or light coming from rooms where the objects are stored or the object

moving by themselves have been reported. Jewelry, wall clocks and furniture are some of the most common haunted objects as well as swords, books and lanterns.

Apparitions of transportation systems include ships, carriages, busses, bicycles, trains, planes and automobiles. There is usually an association with a tragic incident resulting in many people getting killed. Sometimes the vehicles re-enact their final

seconds as a ghost ship or ghost train that appears periodically. Stories of ghost ships that appear out of the fog to warn of impending doom or of train wrecks that occur long after the tracks have been removed from a town are not uncommon.

What About Poltergeists

The term Poltergeist is a German phrase which translates loosely into "noisy spirit" or "rumbling ghost". Noisy ghosts have been recorded in history as early as Ancient Egypt, where stones rained from the sky and beds were shaken. Recently, mot poltergeist activity seems to be centered in Great Britain. Reports of mischievous or even vengeful spirits moving object, making noise or odors are common. Other activity includes making objects disappear or throwing dirt, rocks, stones or other items. In Auburn, Washington, employees of the Fred Meyer store reports shoes being rearranged and even being thrown at employees and customers! Some poltergeists have been known to make noises or even speak and sing, as in the Bell Witch report of 1817.

This disturbing activity can last for a few hours or a few years. It starts and stops suddenly, making it difficult to predict or investigate. The sometimes violent activity seems to be centered on one person, who parapsychologists call an "agent". When the agent is not present, no activity takes place. This gives rise to the hypotheses that the agent is actually creating the poltergeist event as an outward manifestation of psychological trauma. This trauma is coupled with the individuals' psychokinetic ability to create the effects.

Most of these agents seem to be females below the age of 20 who are normally not aware that they are directing the activity. There does seem to be a link between the agents and their state of mental or physical health or emotional changes that bring about anxiety, anger, hysteria and phobias. For this reason a sound understanding of psychology is encourage for any ghost hunter working in this arena.

There are differences between a simple haunting and poltergeist activity. Hauntings involve ghosts of deceased beings who appear frequently, and the appearances occur in areas that the spirit was familiar with before their death. Hauntings are normally non-violent and occur continuously in the same general area over time.

Poltergeist activity can become dangerous both mentally and physically. This type of activity may not be ghosts at all, but mass forms of psychokinetic energy of a living person who is unknowingly controlling the activity. This activity can be triggered by the agents' trauma in any location at any time. Poltergeist activity seems to build up over time to a climax, disappear and then start all over again.

The Bell Witch haunting occurred between 1817 and 1821 and was associated with a man named John Bell. These events were witnessed and documented by hundreds of people, including Andrew Jackson. According to the story Kate Batts believed she was cheated by Mr. Bell in a land purchase and swore on her deathbed to get even. After she dies, the haunting began. Some even claim that the death of John Bell was caused by Kate, and at his funeral it is said that Kate sang loudly and joyously.

In 1958 a poltergeist caused liquid to spill and caps of bottles to pop off with a loud report. This did not occur in a drafty castle or old monastery, but in a green ranch-style 3 bedroom home just 30 miles from New York City. The home was built in 1953 and the event became the first haunting that was actually shown on television. Dishes vaulted from the kitchen cabinet to shatter on the floor and a night table flipped over in the sons' room. A bowl of flowers slide down the dining room table and a bookcase turned end over end in the basement. In total, a record of 67 recorded instances occurred between February 3 and March 10. Building inspectors, electricians, plumbers, firemen and parapsychologists attempted to discover the cause of the events without success. The event was even investigated by the local police but no natural cause could be found.

More recently a loud noise was heard over the July sky in the village of Boqate Ha Sonia in Africa. One of the village residents saw a large stone smash into the cooking area in front of her house and knock over and crack a plastic container. Thinking that it must be a poltergeist, she sprinkled holy water around her house and on the stone, and no more stones fell. Other residents had stones bounce on their roof and kept the stones as proof. When investigators from the

National University of Lesotho investigated, they collected over 400 different stones which turned out to be… meteorites.

Other plausible explanations to poltergeist activity include the most simple; a hoax. Many investigators are frustrated after spending considerable time and effort researching a haunted location where the events simply do not reproduce themselves for the investigator. Many "agents" have been caught by investigators in the act of throwing objects, and a few of the "agents" have confessed to faking the events for a variety of reasons. Some create the hoax for the attention, some to challenge ghost hunters and to embarrass or discredit those who explore haunted locations. The longevity and consistency of the poltergeist reports makes this topic a source of discussion among ghost hunters, paranormal investigators and parapsychologists alike.

What has consistently been reported at ghost sightings?

When someone sees a shadow on a wall, it may be just that- a shadow on the wall caused by a passing car or airplane. Sometimes, there is no passing car or airplane. When that shadow is accompanied by other events such as a bump in the night or lights being turned on or off, the chance of ghostly activity increases. Some of the things that have been reported at ghost sightings or hauntings are outlined below:

- Shadows and fleeting shapes may be caught out of the corner of the eye. Some times the shadows have a human form while other times they are simply dark shadows. Feelings of being watched are not uncommon when ghosts are around. If the feeling comes and goes consistently in a specific part of the house it may be significant.

- Animal reaction has been reported such as a dog barking at something unseen, a cat hissing at a corner when there is nothing there. Animals have sharper senses than humans and have been reported to be watching something across the room that is invisible to their owner.

- Unexplained noises are commonly reported such as the sound of footsteps, knocks on walls or wood, banging, rapping; scratching sounds or the sound of something being dropped. Cries, muffled voices and whispers may also be reported, as has music coming from an unknown source. Some people report hearing their names being called. Unexplained odors and smells have been reported such as the odor of a cigar or perfume. Foul odors such as something rotten have also been reported during an event.

- A sudden chill or change in temperature - cold spots are classic haunting symptoms, but any instance of a noticeable variance in temperature without a discernable cause could be evidence.

- Doors, cabinets and cupboards opening and closing when not being observed directly are sometimes associated with these events. The observer may hear the sounds of the door or return to a room to find a previously open door closed that had been left open. Lights or appliances may turn themselves on and off. Any electrically powered item may become energized and begin to operate, or turn itself off unexpectedly.

- Small items may disappear and reappear at a later time or place. This is sometimes referred to as "the borrowers' phenomenon". For example, a check book or set of keys is missing. A search for the item is fruitless. The item is later found in the middle of the floor or table that had been previously searched, sometimes days or even weeks after the item was noticed to be missing and searched for.

- Feelings of being brushed or touched by something invisible may be experienced. Touching the hair or face or putting a hand on the shoulder may be reported, while others report feeling a gentle poke or nudge. Some people in bed report that they can feel or hear someone sitting on the edge of the bed. Physical assault such as scratches, slaps and being shoved are rare.

- Moving objects such as glasses or plates sliding across the table, pictures falling off walls and furniture sliding across the floor have been reported.

- Apparitions may appear in the form of an orb, mist or even a human form that is transparent or disappears quickly. Manifestations may include unexplained writing on paper or walls or handprints and footprints.

The presence of some of the events discussed does not necessarily mean that the place is haunted. There may be a perfectly rational explanation for the phenomenon. The human mind and senses can be fooled easily and can lead people to jump to conclusions. The ghost hunter must rule out as many rational explanations as possible so that the truly unexplained phenomenon may be examined in detail. Natural or man-made explanations may include:

- Noises could be caused by the house settling on its foundation. Plumbing and toilets may run or drip while squirrels and mice may scamper within the walls of the house.

- Borrowers' phenomena could just be carelessness and forgetfulness.

- Shadows could be just that - shadows caused by a passing car's headlights, the lights from an airplane or illuminated business sign.

- Doors closing or opening or objects seeming to move by themselves could be explained by uneven floors, tables or even door hinges that have been installed incorrectly.

After examining the possible natural causes for the unexplained activity, if the observer can find no adequate natural explanation a search for "unnatural" or paranormal explanations may be in order.

People who experience a ghostly event will swear that these events are not the product of their imagination. The more extreme that the phenomenon is, the more the person will be convinced of the authenticity of a ghostly sighting. If the event is witnessed by more than one person it takes on greater credibility. Physical evidence such as photographs or recordings also lends credence to such an event. If the event occurs periodically, that is, repeats itself again and again the person experiencing the event should keep a journal. If strange things continue to occur after ruling out rational explanations for the phenomena that are taking place people should document them. A journal of the phenomena should be maintained as the events occur. Record the 5 W's (Who, What, When, Where, Why).

Write down the times, weather conditions and circumstances when something takes place as well as anyone who is in the immediate area. For example:

June 2, 2002; 10:30 p.m. – John B and Julia C were sitting in the front room on the couch watching television. The bathroom light switched on by itself. John went in and turned it off again. No one else was in the house; the weather was clear and calm.

June 10, 2002; 9:14 p.m. – Bob K was in the kitchen below the upstairs hallway preparing a meal using the stove and pots and pans. No one else was in the house. He heard footsteps crossing the upstairs hallway again. No one was up there. Went up to investigate and could find no cause. There was a light rain falling outside and it was dark.

Unexplained noises should be recorded with a tape recorder. Use a recorder with a hand held microphone, not the internal microphone on the tape recorder, since the internal microphone will pick up the sound of the machines own electric motors. Some investigators address the ghost by speaking aloud to the room, asking for permission to record its voice and if the ghost has anything it would like to say. Record for about 30 minutes and then listen for any unusual sounds on the tape that cannot be accounted for.

Physical phenomena should be recorded using photography or videotape. Keep the journal, recording and camera equipment handy to document the phenomena as it happens.

What's the deal with orbs?

On photographs of a haunted area there will often be seen circles or globes of light. These are called orbs. Orbs are commonly believed to be some form of energy. Some feel that an orb is a dimensional transportation device for energy beings. Others feel that orbs may be alien beings, spirits or some type of dimensional transporter. Orbs may appear to have colors associated with them such as transparent or blue as well as different shades of intensity. In some pictures you may catch orbs with a nucleus in them- this is the heart of the orb. Some orbs even have smiling or grinning faces in them.

An orb or globule is a term used by paranormal investigators to identify energy caught on film. Investigators are not in general agreement about what they are. Orbs may be individual spirits or even beings engaged in astral travel. Some investigators feel that an orb may be part of a ghost, rather than a complete ghost. Others feel that the orbs may herald the approach of ghosts and are not part of the spirit at all.

Orbs appear to respond to humans and possibly other creatures. The same may orb follow a photographer around throughout the evening. Orbs can move at an amazing speed, which is why they are sometimes referred to as "Speeders". Orbs may be naturally curious, just as we are when we are living. They know what you are doing when you are trying to photograph them; some may be camera shy, and some are just downright camera hogs!

Uninformed investigators will easily mistake lens, sun spots, dust or rain, and claim that this is proof of paranormal activity. A true Orb must be distinct and is different than dust, pollen, or water spots. Investigators must rule out dust, rain, sun spots and lens distortions when evaluating orb photographs.

The images below were taken in Tucson Arizona in 2005 outside the Crystal Palace Saloon. There is an orb in the image on the left, and the image on the right is a control photo taken, where there is no orb.

Ectoplasm
Ectoplasm is found when a spirit has stopped traveling and is standing still. It is in this instance that the energy of the Spirit retains a density that resembles white smoke or fog.

Apparitions
An apparition is the physical form of a person who is no longer living that appears either to the naked eye or on film. Ghosts or spirits can appear as an apparition to the living. When an apparition that shows up on film that was not seen when the picture was taken is considered to be a ghost. Visiting spirits do not usually feel the need to announce their presence by allowing you to photograph them the way they once were, and they are not obsessed with how they used to look in their physical body. A ghost only remembers what it wants to see, and it appears in the period dress and physical body that it still thinks it inhabits.

Portals
Some investigators believe that there is a "Gatekeeper" that sometimes observes activities around the portals. Portals actually make an audible noise similar to a crashing sound when they open or close. This crashing sound has been heard by many people- it may

sound like it is coming from another room in the house, or from the immediate vicinity.

Some investigators have noticed what sounds like a "knock knock" sound before they receive extremely clear voices from unknown entities. They refer to this sound as the "portal knock". This double "knock-knock" may be what is captured when someone is speaking to us while coming through the portal or when talking to us while still on the other side in their spectral realm.

A portal seems to be a doorway to another dimension. Think of a portal as being the spectral taxi that picks up and drops off spirits; whether it is a Spirit visiting our plane or someone who has just passed on- the portals are there. Portals can open anywhere, but are more common in cemeteries where it is quiet, and where entities and spirits can come and go without disturbing the living.

Definitions of vortexes vary. Some use the word to describe the tunnel where spirits can pass through to our dimension. Others refer to this as a portal. However, a vortex is always the same on film- it is normally a tube-shaped anomaly. This may be the manifestation of a system used to travel from the spectral realm to our earthbound material realm. It may also be the opening that would enable an earthbound ghost to pass through the white light as some sort of tunnel. This is why ghosts will sometimes indicate that they have seen the light, but have refused to go into it.

Communicating with the dead-EVP

Ghost hunters use the acronym "EVP" which stands for Electronic Voice Phenomenon. This is an event where tape recorders have been demonstrated to record voices and sounds associated with the dead. Using a tape recorder, the ghost hunter records the sounds around them and then replays the tape at a later time and sometimes finds sounds or voices on the tape that were not noticed at the site.

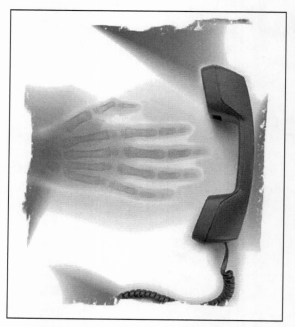

The sounds of entities that are picked up on our cassette and video recorders that were inaudible at the time of the recording are EVP.

EVP also refers to sounds of residual hauntings- bed springs creaking in a now empty wartime hospital room, unseen piano music and so on. EVP's are considered to be one of the most positive piece of evidence that an investigator can obtain.

Recording the dead using electronics have been reported for quite some time. As electricity was being discovered at the turn of the century applications were developed for this new science. In 1915 David Wilson built a device that was sensitive to electrical fields. He noticed that the needle of the device would move during his sittings and recognized the pattern of these movements as international Morse code. When the code was translated it appeared that communications were coming from beyond in both English and Russian.

In 1920, F.R. Melton developed a device that he dubbed "a Psychic Telephone". Thomas Edison was quoted in the Scientific American journal as saying "I am inclined to believe that our personality hereafter will be able to affect matter. If this reasoning be correct, then, if we can evolve an instrument so delicate as to be affected, or moved, or manipulated by our personality as it survives in the next life, such as an instrument, when made available, ought to record something." When he died in 1931 it was reported that he was working on a project to develop a machine to communicate with the dead.

In December of 1956 two men captured the first recordings of the voices of the dead. Attilla Von Szalay claimed to be a natural medium and his co-discoverer, Raymond Bayless was interested in the occult. They rented a studio and Attilla meditated in a specially designed cabinet which was connected to a sensitive microphone and an amplifier. After what they thought was an unsuccessful session they played back the tape and were surprised to hear distinct voices.

Three years later, in 1959, Friedrich Jurgenson was wandering through the woods in the Swedish countryside taping bird songs. He was a producer of documentaries and when he played back his tape he heard a distinct low male voice lecturing on bird songs. The voice even emphasized the differences between the birds' songs at day and at night. Jurgenson was fascinated and attempted to recreate his result with different backgrounds and recordings of any naturally occurring sounds. He reported that his recordings contained voices claiming to be his own dead relatives, including one voice from his mother in which she call him her "Little Freidel" (his childhood nickname) and claimed that he was being watched from the other side.

Jurgenson joined forces with Latvian Psychologist Dr. Konstantin Raudive in 1965. They discovered that results could be improved if some kind of background noise or carrier wave was provided such as radio static. Jurgenson theorized that the voices were able to manifest themselves through an altering of the sound waves. He continued to experiment and his results included some very personalized messages using his name and the names of his deceased relatives. This personalization helped to eliminate the possibility that he was simply picking up stray radio signals.

How EVP works

Modern ghost hunters classify sounds caught on tape into three types. They tend to have a rapid vibration and a peculiar rhythm associated with them. Sentences tend to be delivered in a monotonous manner. Individual words are delivered rapidly, but the pauses between the words are of natural length.

Class A is a message that can be generally understood and heard without headphones. Voices tend to be the loudest of the three types with the vibrations making up the words. The words do not diminish as they do with the other classes of voices. Many researchers feel that the entities sending this type of voice have fine tuned their ability to communicate. When classifying EVP is it important to remember that a loud EVP does not necessarily make it a Class A EVP. It must be understood.

Class B voices are reported when pieces of the words tend to fade in and out and require headphones to be heard. The volume is lower than class A and it becomes more difficult to determine what is being said. The voices can be interpreted differently by various listeners because of the lesser quality of the sound.

Class C voices require headphones and are almost whisper-like with an overall faint quality going in and out of range. This type of recording often requires amplification and filtering to be understood.

The basics of EVP recording

To record EVP the researcher must be prepared to contact the other side with an accepting attitude and a serious demeanor. The surroundings should be free of distractions so that the researcher can focus on a receptive state. Some feel that the researcher should be in a place of significance the being they are trying to reach.
Cemeteries are reported to work well because they are quiet and the atmosphere is reverent- prime conditions for this type of activity.

EVP often involves a lot of time spent listening to audio tapes to find a short message from beyond. This may be compared to looking for a small piece of gold in a stream, it's there but it takes a lot of patience to find it.

The researcher should have a tape recorder with a microphone jack, a tape counter with a push button reset and an external microphone that is designed to record a high frequency (lowest number of Hz and highest number of kHz) range of vocals. The microphone should be omni-directional to catch the sound from around the area, not a uni-directional microphone that records from one direction only. Use fresh high bias cassette tapes and have a set of headphones that are large enough to cover the entire ear.

Most recordings require that the tape be played later. A recent development in technology is a three head recorder that allows the technician to hear the recording as it is being made. Some digital recorders have this same feature, allowing the person who is recording the session to review the session as it is being recorded.

When ready to begin recording at the location, insert the new unused tape into the recorder and zero out the tape counter. Attach the microphone to the microphone jack and turn on the switch of the microphone if it has one. Press play and forward to move the tape past the tape leader, and then stop the tape.

Position the tape recorder near you with the microphone as far from the recorder as possible. Press record and ask for communication from the other side aloud. You may want to mention the date and time and ask any specific question you would like. Allow plenty of time between questions, and have the tape run for three to five minutes. Thank the spirits for their cooperation and stop the tape.

When ready to listen to the EVP, rewind the tape and put the headphones on. Turn the volume up to the loudest setting that you can stand while still being comfortable. Concentrate on the hiss or the white noise and note the counter readings for any fluctuations in the hiss. Replay those sections where you found fluctuations in the hiss to try and pick apart anything in the sound fluctuation.

Other types of electronic phenomenon use a variety of electronic methods. Some researchers believe that the spirit needs some form of a carrier wave to project their voices onto, very much the way our voices are transferred by radio.

In the early days of radio the pioneers such as Morse discovered that a radio wave could be generated and sent out by an antenna on a specific frequency. By creating an electrical spark the carrier wave was disrupted. Morse used this discovery to develop a method of communication called Morse code which used a series of long and short spark gaps that correlated to long and short dashes used in his code. Not long after, other researchers discovered that instead of disrupting the carrier wave, it could be modified. They attached a simple carbon microphone to electrical leads that fed the carrier wave, and then broadcast the modified signal. At the other end of the signal an antenna picked up the altered wave and fed the altered signal through another carbon speaker and the sound successfully emerged that was similar to the one that was sent. When using traditional radio signals the antenna creates this carrier wave.

Researchers feel that by providing some form of carrier wave the investigator can obtain more EVP. This may be accomplished using radio waves, or sound waves, known as white noise. The theory is that white noise provides some form of wave that can be manipulated to effect communication. White noise can be electronically generated, or sometimes background noise such as running water or even jet engines flying overhead can be effective. Telephones carry our voices over a wave type system and there have been rare reports of this type of occurrence. That would be a long distance call!

Investigators have used video feedback where they create a loop with a video camera and a television and video tape recorder to allow the dead to manipulate the signals created by the feedback loop. This may allow images to be shown upon playback. Experiments have been performed where spirit contact is requested using a computer that had been turned on and a simple text editor that was open and running during the designated time.

Natural Explanations

While the thrill of the hunt itself can be rewarding most often ghost researchers discover natural explanations for the paranormal research that is being investigated. This may be discouraging to new ghost hunters who seek to catch a spirit, put it in a jar and display it to the world as evidence or proof. In actuality, it is the job of the ghost hunter to investigate reported instances of ghostly activity and weed out those natural or man made explanations in a scientific manner as often as possible. Once these explanations are made and cases are classified the ghost hunter is left with a small percentage of cases that are truly unexplained. These unexplained cases are where new research must be conducted. Researchers must also be aware that there are many people who enjoy the popularity and publicity attached with ghost haunting. Some people may falsify instances or exaggerate claims in an effort to raise publicity for themselves. Some even claim paranormal activity in an effort to boost business ventures such as a "haunted" bed and breakfast or tavern.

Experienced researchers are painfully aware that if they do not address the natural explanations that could account for a spiritual sighting one of the readers or a member of the general public will most likely jump on the situation and the entire case begins to look like a fools exaggerated report on ghosts. The media loves a circus! In other words, if the researcher does not explain the natural reasoning of a sighting someone else will. So the investigator should address likely explanations as well as any unnatural results or findings.

Orbs

Orbs are often seen in photographs as circles of light. Sometimes these balls of light are merely dust particles floating in the air. Some technicians will use a high power (million candlepower) light to shine into the area to identify dust motes and particles floating in the air that may not be viewed by the observer. In a trip to Tombstone, Arizona for example the orbs seem to be everywhere in the town. On closer inspection the town is located in a dry, dusty, southern portion of the United States and the dust is everywhere. This does not mean that there are no actual ghostly orbs in Tombstone. It does mean that the investigator must take extra care to identify orbs from dust particles and separate those photographs from photographs of actual orbs.

Weathermen and newspapers normally report the relative humidity in their reports, but he public seldom understands the effects of this index. Simply put, relative humidity measures the amount of water vapor in the atmosphere. This relative humidity can't normally be seen, but when the humidity approaches 100% the water vapor begins to condense and become fog, which may be misinterpreted as a spirit attempting to communicate or possibly as ghostly ectoplasm. When humidity is below 100% it may condense on dust and particles causing the particles to swell. This swelling redirects sunlight and produces a haze or possibly orb images in pictures.

Noises
There is nothing spookier than ghostly groans or moans coming from a deserted graveyard or castle. These noises can be difficult to track down but can sometimes be attributed to wind moving across a hole in a stone wall, passing through boards in an old farmhouse or even wind in the trees where a nest has been made by a bird making a hole in the tree. As wind picks up speed and blows across a hole in the chimney a deep moan may be heard.

Water from underground streams or old plumbing may account for some noises that are not readily apparent since the water source is hidden below the ground, behind a wall or beneath the floor board. Modern investigators may not be aware that the old farmhouse that they are investigating once had its own well and cistern to collect water before the community established a common water system. Abandoned sewer systems or septic tanks may still be found on old "haunted" farms.

Moving Objects
Researches sometimes are asked to explain or witness objects that seem to move by themselves or be moved by a ghost.

Disappearing Objects

Investigators often hear about objects that disappear or vanish, only to reappear in plain sight at a later time. The people reporting this type of activity often claim that the object was taken by a ghost and may have had special significance to the ghostly suspect.

Sometimes the item that has been reported to have vanished was simply misplaced. Most of us have misplaced our keys or wallet at some time, only to find them later on in a clearly conspicuous place.

Observed Spirits

Being able to view a spirit is one of the ghost hunters' greatest joys. Spirits have been viewed on video tape and in photographs and reports of sightings at graveyards and other haunted locations are some of the things that make ghost hunting a popular past time.

Low Frequency Sound Theory

Low frequency sound waves may be generated by geological activity, wind or solar storms. These sound waves (sometimes referred to as infrasound) may causes effects that are similar to everything associated with a haunting. Low frequency wave generation may be demonstrated by blowing air across the mouth of a glass bottle containing water and observing the sound. The less water in the bottle, the deeper the sound appears. Replace the bottle with a cave entrance with wind blowing across the opening one can see how this effect can be produced naturally. Some sounds may be so deep that they range into infrasound ranges that are too low to be perceived by the human ear, yet still affect the area. It is difficult to measure infrasound due to the fact that it vibrates at a frequency below the level of human hearing.

Stereo systems in the home demonstrate the concept that low frequency sound is not very directional. The sound may be heard regardless of location, while high frequency sounds, such as a high cymbal crash can be pinpointed more easily. Bass sounds seem to come from everywhere.

Evidence suggests that low frequency sound can cause human beings to hyperventilate and even causes vibration in eyeballs. Other responses include anxiety and apparitions. Researchers should be aware of this type of sound and seek answers to why some people are affected and others seem to be immune. Research continues in this field with the military even considering the potential use of Infrasound as a weapon. The shortfall of a weaponized Infrasound projector is that the sound is not directional and would tend to affect friendly as well as hostile combatants!

Vic Tandy has explored the effects of infrasound on human beings and has published a paper for the journal of the Society for Psychical Research (Ghosts in the Machine and soon to be published Something in the Cellar). In a 14th century cellar near the Coventry Cathedral people had reported a "presence which frightened them. Some felt that they were intruding or disturbing something when they entered the cellar and others reported seeing the face of a woman. Using very precise instruments, Vic Tandy measured the infrasound at 18.9 Hz. He recognized that this low frequency is below the range of human hearing but that it may cause people to react negatively as they hyperventilate. The sound actually caused vibration in their eyeballs which affected their vision. He started investigating infrasound at a laboratory where a janitor had quit; complaining of a grey object she saw out of the corner of her eye and the room had gone cold. Tandy was working late one night when the grey thing came for him and the hairs on the back of his neck rose. He turned to face it and it disappeared. The next day Tandy was working on a foil for an upcoming fencing tournament and the blade started to vibrate while clamped in a vice on a workbench. He knew that there must be a scientific explanation.

Upon checking around the room he found that a new extractor fan had been installed in the lab and when the fan was switched off the effects ceased. This may be the beginning of a link for hauntings as well as sick building syndromes. References at the back of this book show where the reader can learn more about infrasound. (Vic, however, hasn't been able to establish the source of infrasound at the Coventry cellar... stay tuned.....)

Cemeteries
Hidden messages from the past

From the earliest days of society mankind has buried their dead. The oldest form of burials dates back four to five thousand years B.C. when the mourners built a tomb called a Tumulus into rock or earthen hills. These final resting places resembled grottos. In cemeteries one can find various types of tombs or memorials. A sarcophagus may be found in cemeteries around larger metropolitan areas in America. This is normally above ground with legs or a round/tapered base. A chest tomb resembles a large container or shipping trunk what has artwork on the

outside. An altar tomb resembles an altar used for worship with more ornate artwork on the outside than is found on a chest tomb.

Ancient Egyptians left writing on the walls of their tombs to let people know who was buried inside. Inscriptions told of the accomplishments of the entombed, who they were related to and the names of their wives and children as a symbol of their importance. The headstones encountered today in a cemetery convey the same purpose.

Headstones mark the ground where people are interred. When walking in a cemetery one may encounter family members who are visiting the final resting place of those who have passed on. A spouse may leave flowers on a gravestone, pat the stone or read the comforting words left behind such as "Loving Wife." Human beings have left memorials to mark their passing throughout recorded history. As time passes, some of the meanings may lose their popularity with modern culture. For example, the swastika was once a popular symbol but after it was adopted by the Nazi party few used it to adorn the headstones of their loved ones. In this method culture changes. The messages are still there, but the meaning may have become hidden with the passing of time.

The modern visitor to old graveyards can read words that are hundreds of years old. These memorials speak to us about an age gone past. Mankind has always formed clubs and organizations around common themes. Some of these organizations continue to thrive, while others may have become extinct. The stones may be adorned with symbols of a culture that has expired. Pictures, drawings, words and symbols etched in stone provide a glimpse into the accomplishments of the person buried there.

The study of symbols found on gravestones is called Iconography. These symbols are etched into stone, granite and marble and left for others to view. Over the years these etchings may become difficult to read, and as organizations come and go, they may lose their meaning to the general public. It may help efforts to communicate with those ancient spirits if one takes the time to learn about the person and that person's accomplishment when the spirit was in the flesh. This section explains what some of those symbols mean.

A **lamb** on a gravestone often represents the grave of a child to indicate the innocence of youth or a reference to Christ being the Lamb of God. Finding a lamb on a stone would indicate that the deceased was a child at the time of death.

The **lions** often found at the entrance to cemeteries and graveyards denote majesty, courage and strength. **Stags** are symbols of piety and their antlers can also be seen to represent the tree of life.

The **dove** is spotted most often in cemeteries in a wide variety of poses. Sometimes it has an olive branch in its beak and is a symbol of purity and refers to the Holy Ghost. **Eagles** denote resurrection and rebirth as well as a sign of generosity. The Eagle was chosen to represent generosity since the eagle leaves half of its prey for other creatures to feed on. Second only to doves in Christian art is the

pelican, which is the sign of ultimate self sacrifice of a parents love for the children.

Dogs are such good companions that people may have then memorialized in cemeteries. In the photo at the right the deceased and his dog were inseparable companions, as depicted on the monument. Sometimes dogs are depicted as the best friend of the deceased, a partner who played a key role in the life of the person.

In Chinese cemeteries **dogs** are said to ward off evil spirits and are guardians of Buddha. The ball under the male dog represents the emptiness of the mind and the female often has a baby Shih Tzu under her paw. Normally a male will be on the east and a female on the west.

Dragons are considered by the Chinese artist to be the ultimate highest spiritual party representing natural wisdom and strength. Sometimes the **Phoenix** can be found on the grave to represent resurrection, transformation and rebirth.

Eyes found on grave markers are an ancient symbol of God and are usually associated with the Masonic order.

A hand coming down from a cloud with three fingers represents the trinity, while a hand in the upward position indicates that the soul of the departed has reached Heaven.

Two fingers pointed upwards indicate that the person was a member of the clergy. Hands held together are a symbol of matrimony. Normally the clasped hands have one masculine and one female arm or sleeve.

An **Anchor** is the symbol of hope. An **Anchor Cross** resembles two upturned anchor ends in the form of a cross that is considered as a reception of matters spiritual. The monument shown here shows that the man was a fisherman who contributed to his community.

Ships on gravestones indicate a seafarer who went down with the ship. As a symbol it may represent the church on its voyage. A broken wheel on the other hand, indicates that the journey is over.

Books are often found engraved on markers and the closed book symbolizes a full life in that the departed has fulfilled the last chapter before passing on. It may also represent the Bible. Open books are used to register the names of the deceased.

Skeletons reclining on a tomb represent passive death, silently waiting for the mortal world to end. A standing skeleton is known as the King of Terrors and is often seen with an arrow, dart, spear or scythe.

Skulls are considered to be the ultimate symbol of death, reminding us that sooner or later death will take us all.

Draped urns are symbolic of the veil between heaven and earth and are common in 19th century graves.

Fraternal organizations

Societies and clubs often had secret symbols that found their way onto the gravestones. Some of the abbreviations found on tombstones may be so old that their meaning has become faded or forgotten. Yet the organization played a key role in the development and life of the person interred and ghost hunters should understand these hidden meanings. This section explains what some of these symbols mean:

FOE (Friendly Order of Eagles) and **Ladies Auxiliary**
This club was stared by a group of theater owners in Seattle in 1898 and was originally called the Order of Good Things. It soon became known as the Fraternal Order of Eagles. Initially it was made up of actors, stagehands, playwrights and theater owners. I grew to a nationwide status to provide brotherhood, health benefits and funeral and burial services.

KP (Knights of Pythias)
Graves of members of this order are distinguished by a heraldic shield and a suit of armor. Sometimes the letters F, C and B are found which stand for Friendship, Charity and Benevolence. This society started in 1864 as a secret society for clerks employed by the

Federal Government. In the 1890's there were close to 900,000 members and recently that number has dropped to about 100,000.

PS (Pythian Sisters)
The female auxiliary of the Knights of Pythias. Their tombstones may have a Maltese Cross with the letters P, L, E and F which stand for Purity, Love, Equality and Fidelity.

BPOE (The Elks)
The Benevolent Protective Order of Elks began as a club for actors known as "The Jolly Corks" in New York in 1866. It soon became a nationwide organization and changed its name to the Elks around 1867. The elk was chosen as the mascot of the group.

AL (American Legion)
This is a group of former service members which was founded in Paris in 1919 after World War I. The group works to provide veterans benefits for service members who are injured, wounded and elderly.

LOOM (Loyal Order Of the Moose)
Founded in 1888, by Dr. John Henry Wilson, this charitable group is known today as the Moose International. The group started with about 1,000 members and this number had fallen to several hundred by the turn of the century. James Davis started selling insurance to members in 1906 with benefits being paid by the club to the members surviving family. By the late 1920's membership had risen to 650,000. Today there are over one and a half million members throughout the world.

WOW
(Woodmen of the World)
Stones or markers in the shape of trees or upright trees mark the members of this

service organization that was founded in Nebraska in 1890 by Joseph Cullen Root. Sometimes the Latin phrase "Dum Tacet Clamet" is found which means "though silent he speaks." It was originally open to members 18-45 years old who were in the woodworking professions. Today there are 800,000 members. Until the 1920's they provided each member with their own tombstone upon death under the adage that "no woodman ever lie in an unmarked grave." The auxiliary for woman was founded in Leadville, Colorado and their headstones often have the words courage, hope and remembrance on them.

NOW (Neighbors of Woodcraft)
In 1906 the Women of Woodcraft, Pacific Circle relocated to Portland, Oregon and changed the name of their organization to reflect its acceptance of both male and female members. In 2001 the group merged with Woodmen of the World with 7,000 members.

MWA (Modern Woodmen of America)
This group is the fifth largest benevolent fraternal life insurance company around with over 750,000 members. They use the colors red to symbolize life and action, green to symbolize innocence and purity of intention and the color white to symbolize immortality.

The MASONS

The Masons, also known as Freemasons, are the oldest and largest fraternal organization in the world. Thirteen signers of the Constitution and fourteen US presidents belonged to this organization. The actual origins have been lost in time, but most scholars believe that Masonry rose from the guilds of stonemasons who built the majestic castles of the middle

ages. The organization was formalized n 1717 with the formation of the Grand Lodge. Masons believe in a Supreme Being and center their lives on their faith, are good citizens and strive to make the world a better place. The Masons included such prestigious members as Benjamin Franklin, Paul Revere, Alexander Hamilton and George Washington.

Commonly found on grave markers of this group are the compass and square as well as the all seeing eye with rays of light coming out which was an ancient symbol of God. Some of the letters that may be found in circles on Masons and Shriners graves may be:

AAONMS (Ancient Order of the Nobles of the Mystic Shrine)
AASR (Ancient and Accepted Scottish Rule)
AF&M (Ancient Free and Accepted Masons)
F&AM (Free and Accepted Masons)
IGGCRSM (International General Grand Officers of Royal and Select Masons)
K of M (Knights of Malta)
RAM (Royal Arch Masons)

HTWSSTKS

(Hiram, The Widows Son Sent To King Solomon – The Shriners) The Shriners were an offshoot of the Masons in 1872. Originally they were only open to 32nd degree Masons. Their emblem is a scimitar blade with a five pointed star and the motto "Robur et Furor" (Strength and Fury).

KT and SOOB (Knights Templar/ Social Order Of the Beauceant)
This group was founded in the year 1118 by a group of monastic
warriors who had been charged with keeping the roads to Jerusalem
safe for Pilgrims. The group grew into a wealthy organization and
was considered dangerous so that in 1307 King Phillipe of France
had them overthrown and took over their lands. The ladies group
was started in 1890 and is known as the Social Order of the
Beauceant. Latin markings of "In Hoc Signo Vinces" are often
found on members graves and translate to "In this sign shall you
conquer."

OES, PHES, ES, PHGCES (Order of the Eastern Star/Prince Hall
affiliated Easter Star)
Started in 1876 this was the female counterpart to the Masons.
Graves of members have a five pointed star with the tip downwards
and a letter at each point. The points are named after the women
Adah, Ruth, Ester, Martha and Electa. Sometimes the middle of
each point will have the initials F, A, T, A, L which symbolize and
oath the women took upon receipt of another degree.

Eastern Star Past Matron
Found on a tombstone with a five pointed star with a link of chain
and a suspended gavel, or a wreath of laurel circles circling the star
with a gavel attached to the chair

RG, IORG, (Rainbow Girls/ International Order of Rainbow Girls)
This group was formed in 1922 for girls aged 11-20 as a counterpart
to Demolay which is for young men aged 11-20. The letters BFCL
are often found in a rainbow with a chain attached to a pot of gold
with two clasped hands underneath signifying friendship. If the
letter R is superimposed over the pot of gold the person was a
member of the International Order of the Rainbow for Girls.

KOTM (Knights of the Maccabees)
This group was almost wiped out by the Stock market crash of 1929,
but was one of the more successful groups to be born out of the Civil
War. The group takes its name from a 2nd century Jewish tribe that
was led in revolt by Judal Maccabeau against King Antiochus IV of
Syria.

LOTM (Ladies of the Macabees of the World)
This fraternal benefit group was formed in 1892 and was the first to be run entirely by women. Tombstones usually have a beehive with a Latin inscription "ad astra per asperi" which translates to "towards the start through adversity."

KC and K of C (Knights of Columbus)
This fraternal organization for Catholics was started in 1882 after the Catholic Church barred its members from joining the Masons. Their symbol was adopted in 1883 and was designed by James T. Mullen who was a Supreme Knight of the Order. The symbol appears as a medieval shield mounted on a cross. Attached to the shield are a bundle of sticks wrapped together around an ax (a symbol of authority in Ancient Rome), an anchor to represent Columbus and a short sword that was used on "errands of mercy" by knights.

IOOF (International Order of Odd Fellows)
The Odd Fellows started in England in the 18th Century as a benevolent and social club for men of the working class. The International Order of Odd Fellows is an offshoot from this organization. This society uses an All Seeing Eye as their emblem, along with two hands clasped in friendship beneath a three link chain and the letters F, L and T. The letters stand for Friendship, Love and Truth. Behind the link on some stones are often found two battle axes on long poles.

DR (Daughters of Rebecca)
A female auxiliary of the Odd Fellows was started in 1851 and considered to be subservient to the male order. A large number of members have dropped off, but their graves are marked with a crescent moon with seven stars to the right. The symbol also

contains a dove (representing peace) and a white lily (representing purity)

GAR (Grand Army of the Republic)
This group is now extinct, but was open to discharged members of the Army, Navy, Marines or Revenue Cutters who fought for the Union in the Civil War between April 12, 1861 and April 9, 1865. Founded shortly after the war by a surgeon named Benjamin Stephenson in Decatur, Illinois the last encampment was held

in 1949 and its last member (Albert Woolson) died in 1956 at the age of 109. The group had 409,000 members in 1890 including five presidents. This made the group a powerful political organization for anyone who was seeking to run on the Republican ticket. Graves are identified by a medal with a five point star with the tip pointing downwards and the letters GAR in the middle. A US flag with two crossed cannon over a stack of cannonballs is above the five pointed star.

SM (Society of Mary)
Found in certain areas of Catholic cemeteries, clergymen are often buried in what is known as a priests circle. A shield with the initials MA overlapped in the middle is surrounded by two flowering vines. Twelve stars representing the twelve founders of the school (congregation) which was created in 1836 by Fr. John Colin and eleven others who were attending seminary at the same time are found above the shield. Beneath the shield is a banner with the phrase "Sub Mariae Nomine" (Under Mary's Name).

CFA (Companions of the Forest of America)
This English based group came to America in 1864. The Independent Order of Foresters broke off from the Royal Order in 1879 at the same time that the Catholic Order of Foresters was founded. The most successful group left is the International Order of Forester.

IORM (International Order of Red Men)
This group started before the Revolutionary War in such groups as the Sons of Liberty. After the war they became the Society of Red Men with a reputation of being little more than a bunch of drunkards. Later the group reformed as the Improved Order of Red Men and in 1885 a women's' auxiliary was formed called the Degree of Pocahontas. The grave marking of T.O.T.E. stands for the Totem Of The Eagle.

Salvation Army
This Christian organization is a quasi military group formed in 1865 by William Booth with the purpose of helping the needy and disadvantaged.

FB (Fraternal Brotherhood)
This group started as a secret beneficial society in 1896 and had considerable holdings including a large building in Los Angeles which was featured on a 1910 post card. The group may have been too secretive, since it no longer exists.

IOBB (Independent Order of B'nai B'rith)
The Children of the Covenant was started in New York in 1843 because Jews were not allowed in any of the other clubs. It is also known as the Anti-Defamation League. In Jewish cemeteries or in Jewish sections of cemeteries the gravestone may be marked with the initials IOBB.

Gravestone Rubbings

Gravestone and monument rubbings were once a very popular way for people to collect beautiful artwork that could be framed and displayed in their home. A stone carver's skill can be preserved, or an ancestor's stone recorded and appreciated through this craft. In some cemeteries where a restoration project is in progress, rubbing may be banned to enable the restorers to preserve the stones. Even if a restoration project is not in progress, if those who care for the cemetery have determined there are fragile stones which may be damaged by pressure applied to the surface of the stones there may be prohibitions against rubbing put in place.

Pre-site work Preparation

Choose your rubbing subject and select a stone that is sturdy with sharply inscribed areas. If the stone feels loose or has obvious cracks in it, do not rub on it so that you do not damage it. Glossy granite and slate usually produce the clearest images. Select supplies according to the result that you'd like to achieve. Pastels tend to be murkier, and smudge easily so they should be protected by a spray fixative before moving the rubbing. Crayon and pencil are more crisp and less likely to smudge, but can abrade the original image.

Check (with cemetery superintendent, whoever is in charge) to see if rubbing is allowed in the cemetery and get permission or a permit. Heavy clothing, high leather shoes or boots, and insect repellent are advisable. Rain gear and a plastic tarp to protect you and your project can come in handy

Gather Supplies
Place the following items in a bag or box to take with you to the site.
- A few gallons of water in old milk jugs to clean the tombstone.
- Paper - thin is better than thick, a roll of white newsprint can be purchased at art shops. A carrying tube to keep your finished rubbing from getting folded.
- Crayons or pencils to make the rubbing with. There are wax crayons made specifically for this purpose, but you can use pencil, crayon, pastels, oil pastels, or kindergarten crayons. If you use pencil, you'll also want a kneaded rubber eraser.
- Masking tape to keep the paper from moving.
- Paper towels to dry the surface and a trash bag to put your debris in.
- A spray fixative to protect your rubbing when you are done so that it does not smudge on the way home. Available at art stores.
- Scissors or a pen knife to cut the paper with.
- A small stiff brush to remove dirt or moss that may be clinging to the stone.

Clean the tombstone
You may have to deal with weeds, thorny vines, poison oak or ivy, or trees, as well as ants, spiders, bees, and possibly snakes. Feel the outer edges of the stone and design and begin by defining the edges and prominent designs.
Don't use shaving cream, chalk, graphite, dirt, or other concoctions in an attempt to read worn inscriptions. Using a large mirror to direct bright sunlight diagonally across the face of a grave marker casts shadows in indentations and makes inscriptions more visible.

Check for any cracks, evidence of previous breaks and adhesive repairs or defoliating stone with air pockets behind the face of the stone that may collapse. Use a soft brush and plain water to clean the stone.

Rub only solid stones in good condition. Don't attempt to rub deteriorating marble or sandstone, or any unsound or weakened stone. If a stone sounds hollow when tapped or is flaking, splitting, blistered, cracked, or unstable on its base you probably want to select a different stone. Stay away from detergents, soaps, vinegar, bleach, or other cleaning solutions when cleaning the stone. Brush gently. Don't attempt to remove stubborn lichen. Soft lichen may be thoroughly soaked with plain water and then loosened with a gum eraser or a Popsicle stick. Clean the stone and dry it with the towel.

Rub

Cut a piece of paper approximately six inches higher and wider than the face of the marker. Leave enough paper around the edge to form a border so you can mat and frame the rubbing when you are done. The paper will keep your waxes from rubbing off onto the stone itself. Stretch the paper tightly over the stone and make certain that your paper covers the entire face of the stone. Hold it in place with masking tape, don't use duct tape, spray adhesives or scotch tape

Start your rubbing at the top of the stone. Rub from side to side with even pressure using large strokes. Use the rounded side of the heel ball or a wax crayon on its side and rub gently. If using a pencil or crayon hold it flat against the paper. Press gently and rub over the entire image until an outline begins to appear. As long as your paper doesn't move you will be able to darken the areas by rubbing over them repeatedly. Brace your free hand against the back of the stone to counter the pressure. You may have to stretch out flat on the ground to complete the rubbing. If you can't rub the bottom markings of the stone, brush away the grass and earth at the very base of the stone.

As the lines and features become more clear, continue to rub, emphasizing the areas where the lines are already visible. Continue to darken in those areas which are most pronounced. When the image is visible on your paper, you have completed your rubbing. The image normally is not as sharp as the original stone. Remove the rubbing and tape from the stone discard it an appropriate receptacle.

Document and finalize the rubbing
Identify your rubbing on the back with the following:
- Name and location of cemetery
- Location of stone in cemetery
- Date of rubbing and Your name and address

Roll your rubbing and place in tube for transport home.

Gravestone Rubbing kits are available from:
www.gravestoneartwear.com 800-564-4310
The Gravestone Rubbing Kit comes complete with instructions and:
- two cupcake-shaped waxes (black and blue)
- 5 sheets of Aqaba brand gravestone rubbing paper (24 x 36 in.)
- natural bristle brush
- special masking tape
- information on becoming a member of the Association for Gravestone Studies

Ghost Tours

For the new ghost hunter there is a wealth of information to obtain about a city or haunted area by taking a ghost tour. These tours are organized by knowledgeable people who have spent considerable amounts of time researching the area to dig up the interesting stories that haunt the area. Some of the tours are walking tours, while other tours include transportation of some type. Ghost tours can be found nationwide by using the internet search engine and doing a search for ghost tours. They are sometimes called ghost walks, haunted tours, walking tours or other creative names. These expeditions can be found in most large cities such as Tombstone, Washington DC, Gettysburg, even Paris, France has a walking tour of their underground tombs, where millions of Parisians are entombed and the spectators walk right next to the stacked bones of the deceased French!

To participate in a tour investigators usually make a reservation in advance and the operator will advise the person where to meet the tour guide. Cameras, tape recorders and other types of equipment are normally welcome on the tours as long as they do not interfere with the tour itself. These tours are very popular among tourists to the city. Dress appropriately for the tour with good walking shoes and perhaps a jacket, umbrella and a flashlight. Some tours meet in the daylight, and then move to more remote locations that may become dark, damp, and slippery and involve climbing old ladders and stairs. Tours tend to last about 90 minutes to two hours.

At the tour site the group is met by their guide. Groups are normally small and consist of not more than a dozen people. Since this is a guided tour all people have to be able to listen to the guide and hear the explanations of what is happening and going on. The guides often dress to act the part. Some dress in turn of the century Victorian garb, others as funeral directors, some even as vampires or gothic characters with flowing capes, top hats and canes. It's all part of the entertainment package and these guides have a penchant for the theatrical. Don't be afraid to ask them to pose with you for a photo or two!

After the group is advised of the safety precautions to be taken during the tour the guide will spirit the group away to their first stop. Along the way the guide will present historical information about the tour, the city and the area that they are going to. Upon arrival at the first stop the guide will present the assembled group with the story of the building, any ghost reports of the area, rumors, legends and other tidbits of information. The group is given a short amount of time to explore the immediate area, take photographs and sound recordings before being ushered to the next area by the tour guide. "Everyone move along, stay together, we're walking, we're walking, we're stalking…"

Ghost tours are lead by guides who take care to ensure the safety of the group as well as to share some of the little known history of the area. Colorful anecdotes of the normal and not so normal people who make up a thriving metropolis add to the fun and excitement of a ghost tour. While there is no guarantee that ghosts will be encountered, participants often come away with tales of "something unusual" that happened on that tour. For this reason ghost hunters often carry their equipment with them in search of EVP or other indications of a haunting. Since ghost tours are limited to the number of people on each tour, advance reservations are recommended.

Some ghost tours involve walking an area, such as the Pike Market Ghost Tour which is offered periodically. This is a light walking tour usually conducted around Halloween by shop owners in the Pike Market. The tour highlights the history of Pike Market and some ghost stories are mixed in with local history to make a fun excursion for tourists. The tours last about an hour and cost about $12. Contact Michael Yaeger at Studio Solstone- 206-624-9102 or 206-682-7453 for details. Another contact is Sheila Lyon at 206-713-8506. (www.marketghost.com)

Another type of tour is the Seattle Underground tour where participants are guided into parts of the city that are normally not seen. (Portland, Oregon also has a tour of this type.) This type of tour is a bit more energetic as the tourists get to climb through old abandoned areas, explore history and learn of some of the more seedy parts of town and some of the ghostly activities that tend to happen there. Tourists gather at a central location such as Doc Maynard's in Seattle where they meet their guide. The guide explains that Pioneer Square has a history of plumbing catastrophes, scandals and misadventures can be found.

Early Pioneer Square, it seems, was built on tidal flats that were regularly flooded with sea water, creating a quagmire that horses and even children sank to their demise. In 1889 Seattle's Great Fire of 1889 leveled most of the city and the founders raised the city streets to provide drainage. These raised streets were eventually covered and enclosed and the lower chambers were eventually sealed off, forgotten and used only by vagrants, bootleggers and women of low repute. At census time the local prostitutes would identify themselves as seamstresses. So the city instituted a sewing machine tax!

This year round tour takes about 90minutes and begins at Doc Maynard's at 608 1st Avenue between Cherry and Yesler in Pioneer Square. It costs about $11 and must be paid in cash. The schedule varies, and is first come/first served. You can get information 206-682-4646 or check them out at www.undergroundtour.com.

The third type of tour is an escorted tour with transportation provided. In Seattle tourists can be escorted in a blood red van by Jake of Private Eye Tours. (www.privateeyetours.com) Jake picks up the participants at stops at the hotels or restaurants and chauffeurs the participants to the sites. The tour involves a minimum of walking and is available year round. The tour takes about two and a half to three hours and costs about $25. Contact Jake directly at 206-365-3739.

The Ghost Hunters

Mission Statement

The ghost hunters' objective is to gather data in a scientific manner which may lead to an advanced understanding of ghosts, spirits and related paranormal activity. This quest for information will take place with a reverence for the deceased and an open mind to theories and methodology. The organizations goal is to collect proof that may bring this study into the mainstream of American life and to assist any individuals having problems understanding or dealing with a paranormal event. The quest continues to provide substantive evidence that "we are not alone". This organization respects the opinions of those who share our passion of investigation in a positive manner.

Code of Conduct

Members of this organization represent not only themselves or the team but the entire organization. All questions or comments from the media, government officials or the public should be directed to an officer of the organization. Failure to adhere to the code of conduct could be considered cause for termination of membership.

Investigations shall be performed in a professional manner with respect to the rights of privacy of the people, families and places being investigated. No damage or alteration of sites being investigated will be tolerated. Investigators must not handle items or property without the consent of the owner. No littering, abusive or foul language, drugs or alcohol is permitted. No weapons of any type are allowed at any activities.

The organization believes in diversity and will not tolerate harassment of any sort due to race, gender, religious beliefs, education level, sexual orientation, personal values and beliefs, family status, age, tenure, physical abilities or appearance.

All investigators must dress in appropriate attire for the physical and social environment of the site being investigated. Clothing should be non reflective and jewelry and loose objects such as wallet chains should be avoided. Cologne or perfumes should be avoided on investigation. Members should wear the official organization shirt or jacket to identify them as part of the organization. Identification badges should be carried by all members.

Investigations will be conducted in a professional and courteous manner under the direction of an experienced team leader. The team leader controls the investigation and makes all decisions regarding the investigation as well as addressing inquiries from the general public or the media.

The organization will not be responsible for lost or stolen items, accidents or injuries.

INVESTIGATION TEAM

A typical investigation team should include:
- Team leader
- Lead technician
- Technician
- Technical observer
- Psychic
- Psychic observer
- Observer
- Videographer

All members of an investigation team are required to submit a member agreement and a member information sheet to the organization. The group will be lead by a team leader who is in charge of the preparations and the conduct of the investigation.

The team leader must be well versed in the organizations ghost hunting procedures as well as demonstrate basic leadership skills. All reports will be submitted by the team to the team leader who oversees the final report for submission to the organization.

With a team of trained ghost hunters the organization can conduct investigations and expeditions to explore the various theories of Hauntings. By structuring these events and associating them with a common goal the team can maintain their focus. The goal of all of this effort, time and expenditure of resources is to develop a library of finished reports that can be shared among the ghost hunting community.

Training for volunteer members

In order to participate in an investigation the team members must undergo basic training in the field of ghost hunting. This is done so that the members can rely on each other and learn as they build their knowledge base.

There are three types of participants in a ghost hunt and each requires their own type of training. When all three types of members agree that something unexplained happened at a particular time and place the ghost hunters have found something substantial. The three types of participants are:

- Observer
- Technician
- Psychic

Observers

Observers are the eyes of the investigation team. All observers should have a camera with them. Observers are trained to be open minded, yet understand the basic concepts of how the human mind can be tricked into seeing things that are natural occurrences and attribute them to ghostly phenomenon.

People tend to see things that they are familiar with. From infancy human beings see the eyes and mouth of their mother in the same configuration. It is no surprise then that people see this same configuration in clouds, mist, dust, fog on mirrors and vapor trails caught on photographs. Reflections on a window or shadows and light playing on a wall may look like an ambiguous face.

If the person is in an agitated or altered frame of mind (having just seen a horror movie) that ambiguous face may become a demonic grin, leering out of the image. This would be a poor observer for the team! Others who see the picture may not see the image at all, or see a fluffy bunny. This "Pattern Recognition Syndrome" is something that observers must be trained to deal with.

Observers must not discount what that they see. They must remain free of judgments and be a witness to the investigation, capturing information that can be analyzed by the group later on.

Suspending an observer's disbelief during a Ghost Hunt is very important. When people seek gold or hidden treasures they must believe that the treasure is there in order to find it. If one believes that they can pan small amounts of gold from a stream bed they will have a better chance of finding something hidden within the rocks and pebbles. Stage magicians face this effect every time that they perform. Audiences know that they are about to be tricked to believe that the magician actually possesses magical powers. In order to succeed, the magician must effectively suspend the disbelief of the audience by weaving a tale that lulls the audience into a sense of belief.

Many Americans are told at a very young age that there is no such thing as ghosts. In countries such as Mexico or Indonesia the belief in an afterlife takes a different slant and more people express a belief in ghosts. It is understandable that people in these countries see more ghosts than the typical American does. If people don't honestly believe that anything is present, their chances of observing anything is pretty slim.

For instance, during a recent expedition a group of onlookers were asked to be quiet and keep their distractions down so that the ghost hunters would have a better chance of detecting something. The onlooker wanted to know if the ghost was shy and how did the investigators know that. The ghost hunters explained that they didn't know if the ghost was shy, but that by keeping distractions and noise to a minimum the ghost hunters would have an increased chance of finding an anomaly among the clues.

PROTOCOL FOR OBSERVERS

It is the Observer's responsibility to be the eyes, ears and voice of the investigation. Observers must participate in the Observer training courses supplemented with mock training exercises and job shadowing. Observers are required to wear an officially approved

AGHOST T-shirt or other type of recognizable apparel on all walkthroughs, investigations or any AGHOST functions where the public may view the observer.

Observers must ensure that they are documenting a witness account of all aspects of the investigation. Observers must not be afraid to ask questions that are pertinent to the investigation and the completion of reports. Observers must keep an open mind, balanced with some skepticism on their approach to the event that they are observing.

Observers must carry the proper tools with them at all times during an investigation or walkthrough. Observers must ensure that all their tools are working properly before the start of the walkthrough/investigation. Equipment includes, but is not limited to:

- Recording devices such as a mini cassette or digital voice recorder.
- External microphone
- Camera such as 35 mm, APS, digital still or video camcorder
- Temperature monitors (infrared or digital)
- Lighted pen or other writing device
- Flashlight

Observers must ensure that everything is being recorded correctly as well as complete and submit their reports in a timely manner. Observers also need to take photographs as often as necessary during a walkthrough/inspection.

Observers must be aware of their actions and the reactions of those around them including other observers, psychics and technicians as well as the reaction of the client.

Observers who participate on walkthroughs must not discuss or reveal any information regarding the walkthrough prior to the investigation recap with the client. Observers must use the investigation maps provided to them as a means to effectively record investigative data.

All copies of pertinent data gathered, including video, photo and audio evidence must be turned in to the team leader. Normally the evidence, reports and recordings become the property of the ghost hunting group that organized the expedition or investigation.

Technicians

Technicians play the role of the professor on the Gilligan's Island television series. The entire investigation boils down to science, something that can be measured, recorded and explained. Using scientific equipment the technician records changes in the anomaly and the area that things are happening in. These recorded bits of information may not prove or disprove the particular haunting, but may build a path of scientific reasoning that explains what occurs scientifically at a haunting. Prior to the discovery of electricity and its use in homes mankind had no instruments to measure or detect changes in the electrical current that flowed around them. When Tesla and Edison began experimenting with electricity they designed and built equipment that would allow them to measure and record this new phenomenon. As mankind entered the nuclear age people like Madam Curie and Dr. Geiger developed machines to measure the invisible particles that were involved in their study.

Ghost hunters use new test equipment to try to measure and record ghostly phenomenon. Technicians routinely find test equipment that was designed for a specific purpose (Geiger counter/Tri-Field meter) and apply it in their study as an attempt to apply scientific theory to an investigation.

Technicians must be trained on their equipment and understand what it is they are measuring. For example, radiation counters can detect different types of particles and waves so the investigator should know what may be present in order to try to detect it. There are two basic types of Tri-field meters. One detects changes as the meter is moved, the other does not. A technician with the wrong type of meter will detect all sorts of changes in the electrical spectrum simply by walking around the haunted site. While he may feel that this change is the result of ghostly activity, they are actually recording their own pattern of movement!

Technicians must also realize what factors could influence their equipment and cause a false reading. For instance, tape recorders have recorded ghostly buzzing and sound that could have been attributed to a ghost, since no one hears that sound when the recording was made. Then it was found that the recorder was using the internal microphone of the machine and that microphone picked up the sound of the electric motor of the tape recorder. Electrical spikes have been found by Tri-Field meters that were thought to be signs of a haunting until the technician discovered a power panel behind the wall that converted 220 to 110 volts (all US houses have one of these).

PROTOCOL FOR TECHNICIANS

Most serious paranormal investigative units have at least one person on the team who is capable of not only documenting the environment, but can also provide *quantitative* and *relevant* data regarding the nature of the environment and any phenomenon that may occur. It could be said, then, that the job of a Tech is to quantify or measure the anomaly to help determine the cause of a phenomenon or find alternative explanations. In the event that no *normal* explanation can be found during or after the investigation, your valuable data may be the key to proving a haunting.

In short, the Tech is responsible for the following tasks:

- Seek out and document phenomenon using whatever methods and instruments are at his or her disposal.
- Correlate and maintain any data collected for further review.
- Communicate with the observer(s) during the investigation. Keep them informed of anomalous measurements so that they can accurately document it.
- Look for and suggest alternative explanations for any observed anomalies during and after the investigation.

Psychics

The psychic member of the research team is sensitive to paranormal events using what is commonly called extra sensory perception. Observers will record what the normal person sees, technicians will record what scientific instruments show them, and psychics may be able to complete the picture by providing information that is beyond our normal senses.

It should be noted that everyone has a certain degree of psychic ability. People can be trained to use their ability and in order to be successful psychics must be employed correctly. Investigative teams must use the correct instrument to detect the correct thing and use of psychics is no different. Care must be taken so as not to influence the psychics' outcome of the investigation. Psychics are sensitive in a number of ways and so are able to add information to the investigation. They develop their own means of focus to gather this information.

Untrained psychics hardly ever have a success rate above fifty percent. Statistically any controlled test using psychic ability (telepathy, clairvoyance, precognition, psychometric, etc.) demonstrates that the normal person is incorrect more than half of the time. Psychics on ghost hunts tend to have a higher percentage than someone who is merely guessing. This fact demonstrates that there is increased accuracy beyond the average percentage when using psychics. Psychics, coupled observers and technicians cause a ratio of plausibility to be enhanced. Trained psychics have an uncanny success rate.

Psychics pick up feelings, emotions, colors, shapes and images. Their visions tend to be abstract. Their mind will interpret these psychic flashes. They are normally very creative people who naturally do not enjoy concrete sequential actions. In order to capture what they are feeling an observer should be assigned to record things for them, using a tape recorder or a pen and paper.

The psychic is normally provided with little if any information about the haunting. Such advance information could stain the investigation and flavor the outcome of the psychic report. This contamination can lead to the psychic making false judgments prematurely. Normally a psychic will not use any magical rituals or ask other people to concentrate or control energy patters.

Because a lot of the technician's equipment makes sound when detecting events the psychic should not be close to such equipment. These visual and audio clues could contaminate the psychic's readings and mislead the psychic. Outside interference may distort the psychic's perception.

Psychics have their own time schedule and the team should not attempt to accelerate this schedule. It takes time to do a psychic reading. Sometimes the emotions may overpower the psychic who would have to leave the area and return later, or not at all. Psychics should detach themselves from the emotional imprints of past events.

Psychic investigators must be aware that emotions may mislead them as well. At a murder scene feeling of anger, hatred and violence may be experienced that may be evaluated as a dark feeling of rage of the ghost. However, this feeling may be one that is not directed toward the living, but is in fact the residual feelings of the murderer at the site and not the emotions of the ghost at all! In this case the psychic may be reading energy from a past event that lingers at the site. Psychics usually pick up energy of past events that tend to linger at the site.

Psychics used on investigations must be trained to record all information that they obtain while remaining detached from the imprints of any events that linger at the site. They understand how they process information and how their subtle body-mind responses can influence their understanding of the event.

After an investigation the psychic and psychic observer should provide the team leader with a complete written account of what they experienced in a time line setting. This time line allows the team leader to match the psychics' discoveries with those of the observer and the technician to note any sequential events that may be correlated. The team leader should interview the psychic and record the interview for future reference.

What makes a good final report?

Ghost hunters have a lot of fun with their avocation. Half of the excitement actually takes place during an expedition or investigation. Then the team gathers again to review their findings and weed out any plausible or natural explanations. This way they can boil the report to a final summary of unexplained anomalies. These findings must be codified into a standard format and then published for others to review. The final publication should include photographs and sound or video recordings whenever possible. This makes web publishing a natural for ghost hunters. At the end of this book is a listing of web sites that the reader can visit to review the results of some of the ghost hunters' work around the nation. There are also sample forms that can be used to gather information at the end of this book that leads to a final report.

Final reports should be filed and a good method of doing this is to compile the final reports on computer and transfer each file onto a CD-ROM. This file should include the photographs and sound or video recordings. Digital photographs should include a file marked "unmodified photos." This file contains all of the photos that were taken during the investigation with no enhancement, enlargement or alterations. The same goes for EVP where recordings of sound can be filed without enhancement. These original files can then be examined by other investigators who may want to attempt a different method of enhancement.

Another file would include "modified" photographs and sound or video recordings. These are the photos where the lighting or contrast has been adjusted or where the image has been cropped or enlarged to bring the anomaly into a better light. These images may have circles or arrows inserted pointing out the face or ghost in the picture.

The final report should contain a summary of what was initially reported to have occurred that caused the ghost hunters to conduct their investigation, a description of how the investigation was conducted and any anomalies reported. A time line should be established that reveals events that happened in a timely manner and any correlation among these events. Finally, a summary of the report and final closing thoughts should be provided.

The final report should include:
- ✓ Date/Location/Time and atmospheric conditions
- ✓ Summary of initial report of ghostly activity
- ✓ Team members names and positions and Equipment and tools used
- ✓ Tests or experiments conducted and their results
- ✓ Psychic impressions
- ✓ Activity found during the investigation
- ✓ Natural and plausible explanations
- ✓ Any reported anomaly, Photographs of anomalies
- ✓ EVP/Video of anomalies
- ✓ Closing summary to include probable type of haunting, reasons for haunting, need for further study or investigation and closing thoughts.

Time Lines

As each team member goes through the investigative process they will be recording events which may indicate a haunting. The team leader must be able to put this information together in such a manner as to establish key events that were witnessed by the entire group. If one person sees something, it may be their imagination. Two people may influence themselves. If three persons report similar activity the team has something!

During a recent investigation review a team had a photograph of an open kitchen door to another room. Not visible during the investigation, an image on the photo showed what appeared to be a face at the top part of the door and a hand on the door handle, partially obscuring the door handle, as if the ghost was attempting to pull the door closed. The technician reported fluctuations of the EMF meter in the same location and the team had a psychic with them, but no one could remember when those readings were taken. (Unfortunately, the psychic did not complete the report in time for this investigation, so the team does not know if the psychic detected anything in the room or at what time it was detected.)

Using time lines the three reports could be correlated as follows:

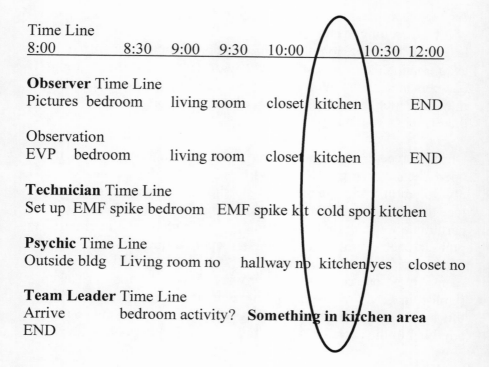

Time Line
8:00   8:30   9:00   9:30   10:00   10:30 12:00

Observer Time Line
Pictures bedroom   living room   closet kitchen   END

Observation
EVP   bedroom   living room   closet kitchen   END

Technician Time Line
Set up EMF spike bedroom   EMF spike kit cold spot kitchen

Psychic Time Line
Outside bldg   Living room no   hallway no   kitchen yes   closet no

Team Leader Time Line
Arrive   bedroom activity?   **Something in kitchen area**
END

Looking at this time line, it appears that at about 10:15, something occurred in the kitchen that was paranormal. The observer got a photograph and some EVP, while the technician found a cold spot in the kitchen as well as an EMF spike. The Psychic felt a presence in the kitchen. Putting all these pieces together there and finding no rational, natural explanation leads one to believe that there is paranormal activity in the kitchen that was documented at 10:15.

INVESTIGATION REPORT

EDELWEISS HOTEL

DATE: 11/14/2004　　　　TIME: 11:30 PM - 12:30 AM

TEAM: (LD=LEAD, PSI=Psychic, TC=Tech, OB=Observer)
Mike W.(LD), Stefanie M.(LD), Merlyn A.(PSI), Darren T.(TC),
Nancy S.(TC), Mark A.(TC), Andrea M.(TC), Guy B.(OB), Kathy
W.(OB), Bryan R.(OB), Christen M.OB), Claire H.(OB), Kay
S.(OB), Larry D. (OB), Jill T.(OB)

RESIDENTIAL TYPE: Business
LOCATION: Leavenworth, WA

WALK-IN IMPRESSION:
Certain team members reported feeling that they were being watched
by someone they couldn't see while investigating the basement. The
gift shop was nice and welcoming while the basement was reported
to feel cold and lonely.

ROOM: Basement
Witness: MERLYN - "I immediately sensed a male presence. I
could see him with light blue overalls and scraggy mousey blond
hair. I feel he is a worker of some sort between the ages of 40-55.
He is not stationary. I feel this man follows people around in the
basement. Marshall, Mike's father, states that he has been followed
and does indeed feel it is a male. This spirit is interacting with
people to get their attention. When people come into this area, they
feel as if they were being watched and they get a bit "creeped out". I
don't feel this is a malicious spirit, but likes having people around."

ROOM: Rack Room
Witness: Several members of the team witnessed the fluorescent
light turn on and off. There seemed to be no explainable cause.

ROOM: Wine cellar corner of basement
Witness: MERLYN - "I physically felt a tingling on my back at the
same time I felt something touch my head. At a later point in the
investigation I again took off alone and went to the corner of the
basement near a sinkhole under the staircase. I felt drawn to this
area. I walked in and felt his presence very strong. As I was walking

out of this area under the fluorescent light, it suddenly turned off. This phenomenon happened throughout the night in different parts of the basement. According to one of the owners this happens to people who go into the basement frequently. Another note about this area, when I stepped into the sinkhole, I heard the song "Werewolves of London" in my head. I don't know the significance of this or if there even is significance to this."

STEFANIE - "I witnessed the fluorescent light click on and then off and then back on again. What was unusual about this was the clicking sound that occurred each time the light would change. It sounded like a light switch, but there were none to be found. The client said that this does happen often and that she does not know of any plausible explanation. Darren and I tested the light and tried to duplicate what we had just seen or heard. We could not do so."

ROOM: Dirt section of basement
Witness: MERLYN - "I was alone in this area when I heard a voice say "over here". I followed to where I felt the voice came from and I found a small shack-like room that had been built. This room gave off a 'creep-out' factor. There are also numerous cold spots. However, this can be explained by drafts from outside." Guy reported feeling a constant cold spot on his left elbow. Marshall reported feeling his hair stand on end. When Kathy took a picture an orb was present in the photo right where he felt the phenomenon. Mostly, the photos shot in this area will contain dust particles. Mark A. reported feeling his heart stop every time he entered this area.

ROOM: Staircase
Witness: MERLYN - "I feel someone standing at the top of the staircase looking down into the basement. I see this twice. I feel that people have seen this at this location. I later found out that one of the clients has seen someone at the top of the stairs before. I also get the feeling there is a missing set of stairs. I feel that were taken out at some point. As I was talking to Kay and Larry near the staircase facing the oil tank, I thought I saw a shadow move near the tank."

ROOM: Main Floor
MERLYN - "As I stand in the basement area, I keep getting the impression of a female worker from upstairs, (main floor). I feel she

was wearing one of those Bavarian costumes that flair out I feel that the area was larger and 'different' than it is now."
Interesting Note: MERLYN - "When we were at the cemetery the next day, I laid down to get whatever impression I could. At this point I started to focus back on this area and NOT the cemetery. I clearly heard a 'BANG'. Then I got the impression of a male and a female with a gun. It wasn't clear to me who shot who, but I clearly felt that one shot the other. I was later informed that the woman that I was sensing in the basement with the Bavarian dress was a waitress when the main floor was a restaurant. She had been sitting at one of the tables and her boyfriend or husband shot her from the street."

ROOM: Goldsmith Store
Witness: MERLYN - "I feel this room was much larger at one time. I can see the woman walking through the wall. I was informed that the wall was built later, after it was a restaurant."

ROOM: Upstairs office of Goldsmith Store
Witness: MERLYN - "I walk into the back office and I get an overwhelming feeling of sadness. I start to feel myself get very emotional and cry. At this point I leave because I do not wish to be seen crying. Mike witnesses this event. I feel something tragic happened here. The next morning the shop owner informs me that the previous owner had had a fatal heart attack in that very spot."

UPSTAIRS/HOTEL
ROOM: Room 207
Witness: MERLYN - "When I'm in my bed at night, I can sense a woman in a long 19th century dress walking down the hallway. I feel this was a 'not-so-nice" part of town in the 19th century. I get the feeling of bordello or 'housing'. The current owner informed me that this was indeed a bordello at one time. At the time, they would call it 'housing' because it was not proper to have a bordello. At about 3:00 am I wake up to the sensation that a female is standing right next to my bed watching me sleep. Then I feel that she kneels down beside me. At this point I clearly hear a woman speaking in my ear."
MERLYN - "Another strong impression I kept getting was the fact that there was a large fire in the town in the 1910's. I felt that it did

significant damage to the town. However, no one I talked to was able to validate that. They were able to confirm that there once was a fire in the hotel, but nothing too disastrous. I still didn't feel that this was the fire I was sensing. Then before I left town to go home, I went to the public bathroom in the middle of town. I discovered a large board that showed the history of Leavenworth. It was there that I found my validation. Written was the following, "Wooden buildings gave way to brick after fire nearly devastated Leavenworth in the early 1910's."

STRUCTURAL NOTES: The Edelweiss was built about a hundred years ago. It has been remodeled several times. The electrical wires running through the building are 6 years old. The plumbing is approx. the same age. Several doors have been boarded up. Stairways that used to lead down into the basement along the outside have been taken out. There is said to be a tunnel that was sealed up but was once used to travel between the buildings. The floors and walls in the basement are unfinished.

CLOSING FEELINGS: Despite the fact there were no unusual technical readings, almost everyone on the team agreed that there was paranormal activity happening in the basement due to individual personal encounters that occurred. The psychic impressions received by Merlyn were all confirmed by the clients.

INVESTIGATION REPORT
TUMWATER BAR & RESTAURANT
DATE: 11/14/2004   TIME: 12:50 AM - 1:50 AM
TEAM: (LD=LEAD, PSI=Psychic, TC=Tech, OB=Observer), Mike
W.(LD), Stefanie M.(LD), Merlyn A.(PSI), Darren T.(TC), Nancy
S.(TC), Mark A.(TC), Andrea M.(TC), Guy B.(OB), Kathy W.(OB),
Bryan R.(OB)

RESIDENTIAL TYPE: Business
LOCATION: Leavenworth, WA

WALK-IN IMPRESSION: Everyone felt very pleasant walking into
the building. The location was very clean and kept up. It was well-
decorated for the upcoming holidays and the environment was very
nice. Earlier in the morning, Merlyn was waiting in line to pay near
the bar entrance. She was drawn to the back area of the bar near the
piano.

BAR: MERLYN - "Overall there is a presence of a large male figure
that wanders in the bar and restaurant area. I felt that there have
been incidences with bar glasses moving behind the bar. I was again
drawn to the back corner by the piano; this area had a very strong
presence. I felt two different energies here. One was the male
figure; the other seemed not to be connected to the bar rather to the
piano. I placed my hands on the piano and saw a young girl playing
it. I also saw the piano traveling up to Leavenworth on a train. This
told me that the piano had come some distance to get here and had
been transferred many years ago. I felt that the little girl is still
connected to this piano and there is some significant activity
associated with it. The owner of the establishment later told me that
there a 'ghost' connected to this piano and she makes herself known
by moving pictures or hearing activity in the piano corner." Kathy
reported witnessing the client revealed that in fact the piano is once
belonged to a young girl. The average temperature of the bar area
was 73-74 deg. F. Stefanie M. picked up a small anomalous EMF
reading near life preserver on wall. The cause of the EMF
fluctuation could not be determined.

DINING AREA: Andrea picked up unusual EMF readings near three lights over the center dining room tables. The readings indicated that the lights were on, except that the lights had actually been turned off a half an hour beforehand. Stefanie M. picked up unusual natural EMF fluctuations in this same area as well. Pictures taken of this area however revealed no apparent anomalies. Possible cause may be faulty wiring within the light fixtures. Kathy captured a picture of a possible orb over the doorway near the back of the restaurant.

KITCHEN: MERLYN - "I feel that most of the activity in the restaurant is concentrated in the kitchen and the prep area for the wait staff. This activity is associated with the male figure."
No anomalous readings or observations in this area.

CLOSING FEELINGS: Despite the psychic impressions, there was nothing substantial found that showed evidence of paranormal activity happening during our investigation. The experiences had by the clients to suggest something unusual is happening in the building. It would be a wise suggestion to continue conducting return investigations whenever possible.

The Equipment

In addition to that "spooky feeling" that people often report, there are events or occurrences that can be scientifically measured which are reported. Paranormal events cause energy disturbances across a wide electromagnetic spectrum. This ranges from the low-frequency infrared through the visible light spectrum, into high-frequency ultraviolet energy, and on to x-rays and gamma rays. Paranormal events seem to tap into existing energy sources to manifest in our reality and disrupt the natural (or background) energy levels. These fluctuations provide anecdotal evidence of paranormal activity.

There are seven main categories of electronic detection equipment used by investigators to capture these energy fluctuations:

- EMF Detectors
- Temperature Sensors
- Static Electricity & Ionization Detectors
- Motion Detectors
- EVP & Listening Devices
- RF Detectors
- Radiation Monitors

Individual Preparedness
Individual members of a ghost hunting team should take care of their own personal comfort and always have a few basic items on them. Good shoes and clothing that is appropriate for the anticipated weather are an individual responsibility.

Each member should bring paper or a notebook, pencil or clipboard and be prepared to contribute to the groups overall experience. A personal time piece (wristwatch) is used to log the time of their arrival and departure as well as to log the times of events observed.

Individual investigators may want to bring along some food and water if their research will take a prolonged time. Ghost hunters must pack their own supplies in as well as pack their own trash out of the area and leave no trace of their visit. Some foods are crunchy or noise producing and these noises must be kept to a minimum. Someone should bring a basic first aid kit.

Individuals should bring along their own personal flashlight with a red lens in case one is called for in the investigation. Sometimes the group leader will ask for members to turn off their flashlights since it tends to blind researchers and it takes a few minutes for their vision to return to normal "night vision" mode. Using a red filter on a flashlight prevents this loss of night vision from happening.

The ABC's of Ghost Hunting Equipment
(Listed Alphabetically)

Camera
35MM Cameras
- More expensive in the long term since you have film and processing costs.
- A negative can sometimes help explain or validate an anomaly.
- X-Ray machines can damage film. Always try and carry your film with you on an airplane and avoid putting it through the x-ray machine, if possible. There are also lead-lined bags available from camera shops that can help protect the film if it must go through an x-ray machine.

Digital Cameras
- More expensive to purchase, but no need to purchase or process film.
- Lack of negative, however, this is not a major downside.
- The better are the digital SLR cameras by Canon, Sony, Nikon, etc. Try and obtain a camera with 3.5megapixles (mp) or higher. 5mp cameras are dropping in price.
- Digital cameras provide instant results because the image can typically be viewed on the LCD screen, which is a major plus.
- Better for documenting an environment because you can typically take more pictures at no cost.
- Easier to store and transport the materials compared to 35mm.

A still camera is one of the most important tools for the paranormal investigator. It can be digital, 35 mm film or a Polaroid camera. Cameras provide visual evidence of a spirit or paranormal phenomenon. Any kind of flash camera will work and it does not have to be expensive. Disposable cameras have been able to produce spiritual or ghostly

anomalies. Expensive and infrared cameras are not necessary and infrared film is also expensive to develop. A camera that does not require manual focusing is the best type of camera to use, as one often spends costly time and energy trying to focus the camera and misses the photo opportunity.

Many investigators use a digital camera. The National Ghost Hunter Society does not mention any preference for digital over film cameras. Digital cameras are very effective at capturing ghostly anomalies and the pictures can be viewed immediately after they are taken. The way a digital camera works is when a picture is taken tiny silicon pixels on the photo recording medium (i.e. a flashcard or something similar) are activated by light and produce an electrical charge, which form the digital image. Since ghosts and spirits are electromagnetic by nature, they often are able to affect electrical devices and the electrical charges that produce the image. As a result, digital cameras capture anomalies such as orbs and ectoplasm more often because the images are electromagnetic in nature as compared to the film camera, which relies on silver-halide crystals for imprinting an image. As with any photographic device, one must

study their pictures carefully to determine what a genuine anomaly is and what may be the result of human error or environmental factors such as dust or moisture.

Most digital cameras have a solid state imaging sensor built into them. This Charged Coupled Device (CCD) sends out a signal (sort of like a sonar wave) that bounces of items in its path and returns to the camera. The photo cell then determines how much light is needed for the flash and adjusts itself accordingly.

Bugs, dust and water droplets floating in the air may account for so many orbs found in digital photography. Closer examination may reveal that the shape of these impurities in the air is slightly different than actual orbs. Orbs tend to be symmetrical, perfectly round and the lighting is always even, regardless of brightness. Dust orbs tend to have a brighter edge on one side or the other and often look egg shaped or triangular. Some technicians will use a high powered spotlight to identify the amount of dust and impurities floating in a room, since they show up readily to the naked eye when hit with half a million candlepower (hand lamps like these can be purchased at marine or boating stores).

In low light situations digital cameras may find a situation where the pixels do not fill in correctly. Kodak, Sony and other companies use the CCD to fill in those spaces with something, which may be considered to be a false orb. Whenever possible, check digital photography with a regular film shot.

When using film, use a high speed film such as 400 or 800 speeds. Experienced photographers may want to try their hand at using infrared or black and white film. When having pictures developed instruct the developer to develop all the images and not take advantage of their "goof proof" development policy. What the developer may see as a poor image may be the very apparition that has eluded ghost hunters for years! Photographers should note the locations of street lights and other sources of illumination so that they do not confuse glowing street lamps as a spiritual orb. Psychic photography tends to be most productive between the hours of 9pm and 6am.

Open film and load the camera after arriving at the location. Use a high speed film of at least 400 speed 35 mm film. 400 and 800 speeds work the best. 1000 speed film develops too grainy and investigators should avoid using it. Black and White film also works well.

Do not smoke or do anything that may create a vapor or cloud, as the smoke may be caught on film and be perceived as a ghostly image. In cold weather the photographers breathe may condense into a cloud and drift in front of the lens. This type of cloud may be considered to be ectoplasm or a ghostly spirit when the film is developed a week later.

Researchers must watch for dust or dirt being stirred up in the area where they are taking pictures since dust in the air can be mistaken for apparitions and orbs, giving a false positive image upon development. Camera straps or even a wisp of long hair of a researcher ending up in front of the camera lens could be considered to be a ghostly spirit when captured on film. Clean the lens frequently and regularly to remove smudges and images on the lens.

Photographers must be aware of reflective surfaces in the area that may reflect such as windows or polished tombstones. The reflected light may look like an orb or other anomaly. Investigators must make note of street lights in the field of vision as well as any other light source locations. They should note the location of other lights in the area that may produce reflections on water, wet or shiny surfaces so that these reflections will not be mistaken as an orb.

Let fellow investigators know when a photo is being taken to eliminate double flashes. This also allows the night scope operators to look away. Night scope operators can get eye damage if they are looking at a flash through the scope. Prior to pressing the shutter release announce "flash" to alert team members of the coming flash.

Follow the hunches of team members. If a drop in temperature is suspected or reported snap a picture. If someone reports seeing something out of the corner of the eye snap a picture. Many people ask the spirit if they can take their picture. Investigators may only get about one or two pictures for every fifty taken. When developing the prints, instruct the developers to process and print every photo.

Load the audio and video tapes at the scene and always use fresh batteries. Set up stationary recorders and let them run or walk around with them. All photographs should be cataloged and archived (along with their negatives if using film).

During audio and video recording, ask questions of the spirits based on what you have learned from the gravestones. Inform the spirits that if they have something to say they can communicate with the team by making themselves visible in such and such a location or by speaking into the microphone. Ask personal questions about their lives. (For example, were you a member of the Masons? How did you die, who left flowers?)

Compass
A compass is used for normal land navigation can detect shifts in magnetic energy.
The compass is the most basic device for detecting changes in electromagnetic fields. A compass may spin erratically when it encounters a field of energy that has a paranormal origin. Deviations from magnetic north will cause the compass needle to point in the direction of the anomaly. Deviations should be 20 degrees or greater to be considered a valid disruption of the magnetic field that could represent a ghostly anomaly. Use natural compasses as opposed to digital compasses.

Dowsing rods
Dowsing rods and pendulums may react to these conditions. Dowsing rods and pendulums can either be purchased at a very reasonable price or manufactured by using readily available items in the household.

EMF Detector
These meters read the electromagnetic fields in an area. It is a common theory that spirits disrupt this field in such a way that you can tell one is present by higher than normal readings with this meter. There are many types and price ranges. You need to be aware of the natural readings in an area or building before you assume that you're reading a ghost presence. Know where power lines, electrical line, major appliances and electronics are before taking readings.

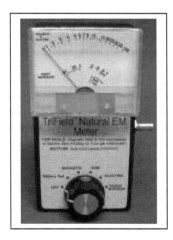

The electromagnetic field or "EMF" meter detects changes in electromagnetic fields. Normal background levels should read between .1 and 1.0 milligauss. Fluctuations between 2.0 and 7.0 tend to indicate the presence of a spirit. Readings outside that range are usually easy to attribute to natural or man-made sources. To be used most effectively, the EMF unit should be swept from side to side and from top to bottom to detect anomalies in the electromagnetic fields. When using an EMF meter, first determine normal background levels in the location being investigated and make sure you are not picking up readings from electrical boxes or electrical wiring. After detecting a ghostly anomaly using the meter photographs of the area should be taken to attempt to determine what is causing spikes in the meter.

Three kinds of instruments are generally used to detect electro-magnetic fields (EMF). They are the electric field, magnetic field, and radio frequency (RF) meters. The favorite for most paranormal researchers are the Multi-Field Meters, which measure two to three of these fields at once. They usually feature a fast reacting needle gauge, at least two sensitivity scales, and are very easy to use. Other meters monitor the combined magnetic and electric field strength and are known as Gauss meters (or Teslameters). The ELF (Extremely Low Frequency) models are best for paranormal research. For monitoring microwave and radio frequencies and also help detect hidden sound or spy equipment, the paranormal researchers make use of RF Meters. It should be noted that all gauss meters, electric field meters, RF/microwave meters, etc. can only measure the strength of the field *at the location of the meter*. The meters can be placed in stationary positions or used like mobile probes while walking around during an investigation. What distinguishes one meter from another is the sensitivity (or the smallest field strength that the meter can detect). For instance, a gauss meter with sensitivity of 0.1 mG (milligauss) is ten times more sensitive than a meter that can only detect down to 1.0 mG. While a more sensitive meter can be successfully used further away from the source of the field, it is still only measuring the weaker field at the *location* of the meter. In looking for a more sensitive meter, compare the minimum sensitivity rating of one meter to another. How effectively a meter can detect a field depends on the strength of the field at the source, the pattern of radiation from the source and the rate that the field decreases with distance ($1/d$, $1/d^2$, $1/d^3$, etc.). Some EMF sources may have symmetrical field patterns, some may not. A single-axis detector is sensitive to the field directly in front of the probe and must be rotated during use to find the proper orientation to the source field being measured to get accurate readings, while a three-axis detector is sensitive all around the probe and is omni directional.

TriField meter can also operate as a motion detector and as a meter that reads static magnetic and electrical energy fields. Be careful of the setting when using the TriField meter because it can also detect geomagnetic energy created from thunderstorms and other electrical disturbances. Before using the EMF detector in the "ghost hunting" mode, check the manual for correct usage. Then take readings around known energy sources such as light poles or electrical junction boxes and appliances to establish a base. Most manuals list the readings that a normal appliance will generate.

Common EMF Meters:
- UHS Meter
- TriField Natural (DC)
- TriField (AC)
- Sperry EMF-200A
- Multidetector II Profi
- CellSensor
- Gaussmaster
- ElectroSensor

Although the presence of AC or DC electromagnetic fields is not in itself proof of paranormal activity, there are several compelling reasons for an EMF meter to be deployed during an investigation. The following are just a few reasons why one may want to document EMF fields at a location:

The presence of strong or intermittent EM fields may be the cause or the byproduct of certain paranormal activity. EM fields may be "feeding" an entity or anomaly.

Strong electromagnetic fields, or even weak or intermittent spikes in these fields, may effect a person's perception and senses in various ways. The presence of EM fields in an area may accompany uncomfortable sensations that are often attributed to a haunting. Strong AC or DC magnetic fields may cause or attract free ions in the air. In some cases, a higher concentration of ions in the air often accompanies ghostly sensations or phenomenon. In these cases the activity may occur more frequently in areas where there are numerous EM fields or magnetized surfaces.

What is an EMF (Electro-Magnetic Field)?
An *electromagnetic field* is a stream of energy that is constantly emitted and absorbed by *charged particles,* such as an *electron.*

An electromagnetic field is composed of two related fields; an electric and a magnetic field. A *charged* particle at rest produces what is called an *electrostatic* field. If the charged particle is undergoing *inertial* motion - that is, the particle is moving but not accelerating - then a *magnetostatic* field is also produced.

A charged particle that is undergoing acceleration emits small packets of electromagnetic energy called *photons* - which are propagating and expanding waves of electromagnetic energy. What we perceive as *visible light* is a familiar example of electromagnetic radiation.

Most EMF meters only detect the *AC* or *DC* magnetic fields produced by charged particles. These sensors use a process called *induction* to produce a current in the meter when exposed to a changing magnetic field. This current, which is proportional to the strength of the magnetic field, can then be measured.

The device is similar to an *electromagnet*, which is simply a coil of wire wrapped around a conductive object (a metal rod, for example). When a current is passed through the coil of wire, a magnetic field is then produced within the conductive object.

The sensor inside an EMF meter is basically the opposite of an electromagnet. It consists of a coil of wire wrapped around a conductive rod. When the sensor encounters a magnetic field, a proportional magnetic field is then produced in the conductive rod, which in turn produces an electric current in the coil of wire. This current is then amplified and measured by the meter.

Induction – Describes a phenomenon by which a <u>changing</u> magnetic or electric field crossing a conductor creates a voltage within the conductor. According to *Faraday's law of induction*, as the strength of the magnetic field passing through a closed loop (a coil of wire, for example) increases, an induced voltage is created in the loop which is proportional to the rate of change of the magnetic flux.

Some EMF meters can also detect the electric field separately from the magnetic field. The sensors used in these meters are simply conductive metal plates. When the metal plates are exposed to an electric field, a current is induced in the plate due to the displacement of positive and negatively charged particles. This current is then amplified and measured by the meter. The current induced is proportional to the amplitude of the electric field.

Detecting RF (Radio Frequency)
Some EMF meters also have an option to detect certain types of electromagnetic radiation. They do so simply with the use of an antenna, which is often mounted inside the meter. An antenna works through a type of induction called *radio frequency induction*. The term describes a phenomenon which causes an alternating electrical current to occur within an antenna when it is exposed to electromagnetic radiation.

Types of antennas
Many antennas are simply a length of wire, called an *electric dipole,* which couple to only the electric field of the propagating electromagnetic wave. An alternating electric current then moves back and forth along the length of the wire when exposed to an EM field. In contrast, a *magnetic dipole* consists of a coil of wire and couples only to the magnetic field of the electromagnetic wave. An alternating (changing) magnetic field is then induced in the antenna which produces a current in the wire.

RF (Radio Frequency) – The RF range is defined as a portion of the *electromagnetic spectrum* which can be produced by an electric current fed into an antenna. This is technically a wide range of frequencies, spanning from 3Hz to 300GHz, and therefore has been subsequently divided into smaller sections which refer to individual ranges of frequencies. Typical RF ranges that these meters will measure include VHF (Very High Frequency) to UHF (Ultra High Frequency), or 30MHz to 3GHz.

Although all EMF meters are designed to detect changes in electric and magnetic fields, most EMF meters are specifically designed to detect *alternating* electric and magnetic fields. These are fields that are rapidly changing polarity, and are typically produced by AC power sources. Some meters, however, can also detect either static fields produced naturally or by DC power sources and sometimes even slowly alternating electric or magnetic fields.

AC EMF meters are designed to measure alternating electromagnetic fields, that is, fields whose electric and magnetic poles are switching (alternating). These fields can typically be found in normal household wiring which alternates at 60Hz (60 times per second) in North America.

DC EMF meters are typically designed to find static (non-alternating) electric and magnetic fields. Meters specifically designed to measure static magnetic fields, such as the magnetic field produced by the Earth, are called *magnetometers.*

The Earth itself produces a static magnetic field of about 30-60 microTesla (300-600 milliGauss). Some static magnetic-field meters, such as the Trifield Natural EM Meter, adjusts, or "zeros out", automatically to compensate for any background magnetic fields. Other meters may need to be adjusted manually to compensate for the background magnetic fields. *NOTE: Biological bodies do not generally posses a magnetic field; however they do produce small electric fields, which can often be detected by some of these meters.*

Many EMF meters have a single magnetic field sensor that measures along a single axis. Since we live in a three-dimensional world, electric and magnetic fields can exist on one or more of the three axis (x, y, and z). What this means is that a single axis meter will only be able to "see" one axis at a time will produce different results depending on its own position within the field.

There may be times when you are interested in obtaining an exact measure of the EM field. To obtain a more accurate reading, it is suggested you position the meter along all three axis and take individual measurements of those fields. These can then be added together using the Pythagorean Theorem.

Three axis meters
Three axis meters have three individual sensors, each positioned along a separate axis. The meter itself then adds these measurements together and displays a number representative of the strength of the entire three dimensional field.

Frequency Weighting
When a human body comes in contact with an EM field, the field will induce a small current in the body. The rate of induction, and the induced current, increases with the frequency of the EM field. Therefore a higher frequency EM field has a greater potential to cause problems with a biological body compared to a lower frequency field.

Because higher frequency EM fields are absorbed more readily by a human body, frequency rated EMF meters will display a higher measurement as the frequency of the field increases, even if the overall energy of the field stays the same. Higher frequency fields are therefore *weighted* more so than lower frequency fields.

Most EMF meters available today are *frequency weighted*, meaning the measurement displayed on the device varies depending on the frequency of the electric or magnetic fields. Therefore, a frequency weighted meter will not always display a measurement that is equivalent to the energy of the EM field, as one might expect, but instead will display a measurement that is proportional to the effect that the EM field would have on a biological body. There are also non-frequency weighted meters available that have a very flat frequency response, and will display a more general measurement of the EM field.

Calibration refers to the frequency at which a *frequency-weighted* meter will produce an accurate (non-weighted) measurement. Typically, this is calibrated to 60Hz to match the AC frequency of household wiring and power lines in North America. Many meters are also offered as 50Hz variations, which is the frequency of AC wiring in other parts of the world. So, if a meter that is *calibrated* to 60Hz displays a measurement of 3milliGauss, then the density of the magnetic field is indeed 3 milliGauss. The sensitivity of the meter will then increase with the frequency until it reaches a peak which varies with the type of meter.

Evidence Bags
Plastic Zip Lock bags can be used to seal and protect any evidence that may be found on the site and prevent future contamination of the evidence. Keep some plastic bags with a pen or marker and some adhesive labels all tucked into one plastic bag for ease of storage.

Flour or Dust
Sprinkling flour or dust around equipment or an area is a method used to verify that the area or equipment has not been tampered with. Investigators must clean up after themselves, so this type of dust must be accompanied with a dustpan and broom for cleaning.

Flashlights
Red filters on the flashlights allow them to be used without destroying the "night vision" of the investigators. Investigators should provide flashlights with fresh batteries. It has been reported at ghost sightings that batteries can become drained quickly and a set of fresh spare batteries should be readily available. Ghost hunters may want to use a red lens cover over their flashlight to conserve their night vision. LED flashlights provide good light at low power consumption and come in various colors. Individual members may want to consider using a camping lantern and bring candles and

matches as a back up. Candles have been known to trigger motion detectors so coordinate their use with the technician of the group.

Gas Analyzers/Testers

Carbon Monoxide (CO) is an odorless gas usually generated as a byproduct of natural gas powered appliances such as furnaces, stoves/ovens, clothes dryers, water heaters, fireplaces, space heaters, or even a leaky grill or barbecue. Carbon Monoxide can sometimes leak into the living area of a home due to a breakdown or decay of the appliance, or the unit's exhaust or combustion system.

Carbon Monoxide exposure can cause a number of health problems including severe headaches, fatigue, cold or flu-like symptoms such as coughing or aching - but without a fever. Occupants may also complain of depression, paranoia, and even audio or visual hallucinations such as voices, footsteps or other strange sounds.

Sudden death or degeneration of normally healthy plants within the home can also be an indication of gas leakage. Anyone who owns a gas furnace should really already have or purchase a carbon monoxide detector. These items are generally inexpensive and can be found in any hardware store. Handheld CO meters that measure the exact concentration of carbon monoxide gas generally cost around $200.

Natural Gas is actually an odorless gas. The utility companies, however, add trace amounts of a chemical called mercaptan before the gas enters the distribution pipes. Mercaptan has a distinctive 'rotten egg' odor, which should make it easily identifiable. Nausea, diarrhea, loss of appetite, dizziness, disorientation, headache, excitation, rapid respiration, drowsiness, labored breathing, anesthesia and other central nervous system effects are common. Natural gas leaks should be easily identifiable due to the "rotten egg" smell. Owners should contact their utility company as soon as possible to find out how to identify and repair natural gas leaks. Natural gas is highly flammable.

Geiger counter and Radiation monitors may be able to detect activity of a paranormal nature. Radioactive objects sometimes emit a greenish light as well as scintillating white sparks (visible only in complete darkness) and more than once have been responsible for alleged "haunting."

Spontaneous radioactive events have been associated with genuine anomalous activity of all sorts. Researchers have found that fluctuations in background radiation indicate a disturbance in spirit energy.

Such radiation may be naturally occurring or

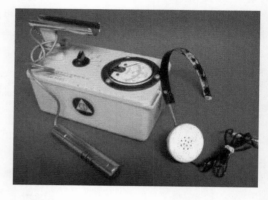

from a leak in an appliance such as a microwave oven. There are several reasons for using a Geiger counter in an investigation:

If the client or other members of the household have an unexplainable illness, they may associate it with paranormal activity. Just like other environmental factors, such as gas leaks, moderate or high levels of radiation can cause intermittent or chronic illnesses. A Geiger counter can help eliminate some of these possibilities. Second, some researchers have suggested a link between paranormal phenomenon and the concentration of free ions in the air. A Geiger counter may be able to explain the presence of unusually high numbers of ions in the environment. Lastly, high levels of radiation can often cause photographic anomalies on film. Testing for ionizing radiation can help explain some of these anomalies.

Geiger counters are instruments designed to detect many of the byproducts of radioactive decay including alpha particles, beta particles, gamma rays, and x-rays. They are just one class of radiation detectors called *gaseous* detectors which are designed around the same principle as the *ion chamber*. Most Geiger counters utilize a gas-filled cylinder or tube called a Geiger-Müller(GM) detector. Any Geiger counter that detects low to medium levels of

Beta, Gamma, and X-Ray radiation. Some meters also detect Alpha particles at close range as well. Do not use meters that utilize an "Ion chamber" instead of a Geiger Muller tube. These are typically called "field meters" or "fallout meters".

Radioactive Decay Overview

The atoms of many elements come in multiple variations called *isotopes*, where the atom itself varies only by the number of *neutrons* contained in the *nucleus*. More technically defined, an isotope is one or more atoms that all have the same *atomic number*, the number of protons in its nucleus, but a different *atomic mass*. The atomic mass number is the number obtained from adding the protons and neutrons in the nucleus.

The variation in the number neutrons in the nucleus of an atom may not necessarily change the properties of the element at all. However, in some elements these isotopes can be *unstable* and *radioactive*. *Stable* atoms are those that do not change or transform over time. By contrast, u*nstable* atoms will often transform or *decay* into a more stable state, and in the process emit varying types of particles and/or electromagnetic energy. This process is called *radioactive decay*. There are several types of radioactive decay, all of which take place regularly in nature. For the purposes of this article, we are only going to discuss a few of these processes. Take a look at the links at the bottom of this article or more detailed information about the other processes.

Alpha decay is a process by which an atom spontaneously releases an *alpha particle*. An alpha particle is basically a fast moving helium-4 atom with two protons and two neutrons. The result is a nucleus with two fewer protons and neutrons. Afterward the atom is typically left in an *excited* state, and releases energy in the form of a *gamma ray* (see: *Gamma Emission*). The alpha decay process is similar to *spontaneous fission*.

Beta decay is the process by which a neutron within the nucleus of an atom spontaneously changes into a proton, or vise versa. During this process a *beta particle* is also released which is either a fast moving electron or positron. Depending on the type of reaction (β^+ or β^-).

β^+ Decay
During this process a proton within a nucleus spontaneously changes into a neutron. A *neutrino (electron neutrino)* and a beta particle, in the form of a *positron*, are also emitted. The atomic mass of the nucleus is conserved, but the atomic number decreases by one.

β^- Decay
During this process a neutron within the nucleus of an atom will spontaneously change into a proton. A beta particle in the form of a fast moving electron and an *anti-neutrino (electron anti-neutrino)* will also be produced. The atomic mass of the nucleus is conserved, but the atomic number increases by one.

Spontaneous fission occurs when the nucleus of an atom splits into two distinct nuclei. The byproducts of this reaction include protons, neutrons, photons (typically gamma rays), and neutrinos. Along with alpha decay, beta decay, and spontaneous fission there are several other processes related to nuclear decay. These include *gamma decay,* also referred to as *gamma emission,* and *internal conversion.*

Gamma Decay (Gamma Emission)
Gamma decay occurs when an atom is in an excited state and spontaneously releases its excess energy in the form of a high energy photon called a gamma ray. Gamma emissions can also occur after spontaneous fission, alpha decay, and sometimes after beta decay. Atoms that can remain in an excited state for a long period of time are called *nuclear isomers.*

Internal Conversion
Internal conversion is similar to gamma decay in that the atom spontaneously releases energy. In this case, however, this excess energy is transferred to one of the orbiting electrons, which results in the ejection of the electron from the atom. Oftentimes, an electron

in a higher energy level will "fall" to a lower energy level and in the process will again release energy in the form of one or several X-rays or an Auger electron.

Radiation Exposure Risk (Overview)
As mentioned above the byproducts of radioactive decay typically include protons, neutrons, electrons, photons, and neutrinos. Many of these emissions can interact with individual atoms and potentially cause damage to biological cells. The dangerous exposure level varies for each type of radiation, but the bottom line is that all kinds of radiation, with the exception of neutrinos, can be dangerous at higher levels.

Alpha Particles
As mentioned above, an alpha particle is a helium-4 atom (two protons and two neutrons) which is typically emitted from the nucleus at about 15km/s. Because of their size, alpha particles are the easiest to block with little more than a sheet of paper. These particles will also slow down quickly in air.

Beta Particles
Beta particles are able to penetrate more deeply and can interact with individual atoms within a body, but can be blocked with a thin sheet of aluminum or lead.

Gamma Rays and X-Rays
Higher frequency photons such as gamma rays are typically the more dangerous kind of radiation. Gamma rays and high energy x-rays can penetrate a human body easily and ionize individual atoms. Exposure to high energy electromagnetic radiation can be especially dangerous because of the massive amount of energy these high-frequency photons are capable of transferring to individual atoms. Significant amounts of absorbed radiation can ultimately result in damage to individual cells and severe burns. A thick lead sheet is generally required to block this kind of radiation.

Neutrons
Neutrons can be very dangerous because they are small enough to penetrate a body, but heavy enough to effect individual atoms.

Geiger counters do not directly detect neutron radiation, and you will not likely encounter significant levels of it unless you are unlucky enough to be caught in a nuclear meltdown or explosion.

Neutrinos
Neutrinos are very tiny elemental particles with a very small mass. They are not charged and in fact only "feel" the weak nuclear and gravitational forces. Because of this and their small size they generally will not interact with a body, and instead simply pass right through it.

Geiger counters are instruments designed to detect many of the byproducts of radioactive decay including alpha particles, beta particles, gamma rays, and x-rays. They are just one class of radiation detectors called *gaseous* detectors which are designed around the same principle as the *ion chamber* (discussed below). Most "Geiger" counters utilize a gas-filled cylinder or tube called a Geiger-Müller(GM) detector.

Geiger-Müller Detectors (GM)
The typical sensor found on a Geiger counter is what is called a Geiger-Müller tube, which is a tube filled with gas - typically neon with a trace amount of halogen - that detects *ionizing radiation*. Ionizing radiation is radiation that is powerful enough to strip electrons from their atoms. In this case a high-energy photon enters the tube and is absorbed by one of the gas atoms. The excess energy is then transferred to one of the atom's electrons which cause it to be ejected from its orbit. A DC voltage is applied to the outer layer of the tube and the center electrode which sweeps the free electron toward the positively charged electrode inside the tube. This creates a small current which can then be measured. The process is closely related to the *photoelectric effect*, which allows solar cells to produce energy.

Most sensors utilizing GM detectors are useful tools to detect the presence and intensity of the radiation, however they cannot determine particle energy levels or distinguish the exact type of radiated particle or photon it is detecting.

End or Side Window GM Detector Probes

End-window GM detectors are typically sensitive to low to medium levels of gamma or high energy x-ray radiation, as well as beta radiation. End-window detectors are generally less sensitive compared to the other types of low-level radiation detector probes. A variation on the end-window probe is the *rotary* or *side-window* design which is often more sensitive due to the larger surface area of the window.

Example side-window detector probe.

"Pancake" GM Detector Probes

Pancake detector probes are also sensitive to low to medium levels of gamma or high energy x-ray radiation, as well as beta and sometimes alpha radiation. These probes are typically more sensitive than the end-window detector, primarily due to the larger surface area of the probe window.

Many of these sensors are designed to detect gamma and high energy x-ray radiation. However, some of them may also be able to detect beta and even alpha particles as well, although their ability to produce an accurate dosage measurement varies. Some probes and meter combinations may only be able to detect the presence of beta and alpha radiation, and not an exact measurement.

As mentioned earlier, Geiger-Müller tubes operate on the same basic principal as the *ion chamber*. When ionizing radiation passes through a gas, collisions can occur which can strip electrons from its parent atom. This produces ion pairs, typically a molecule that has a net positive charge and a free electron.

Similar to Geiger-Müller tubes, ion chambers consist of a cylindrical can filled with a gas, although instead of neon it is typically filled with dry air, carbon dioxide, or some other gas mixture. A DC voltage is applied to the outer layer of the tube or cylinder and the center electrode. This charge repels free electrons away from the walls of the tube and sweeps them toward the positively charged electrodes near the center.

Meters utilizing ion chambers typically measure an average ionization rate as opposed to individual interactions and are typically not as sensitive as those that utilize a Geiger-Müller detector. See the "Field Survey Meter" section below for more information about meters that utilize ion chambers.

Examples of Geiger Counters

Geiger counters come in many shapes and styles – from larger boxy units with analog displays to smaller digital meters. As with any meter, be sure to research each model's specific abilities before purchasing or using it in an investigation.

The "Field Survey" or "Fallout" Meter
Many of the radiation meters on the market today look very similar and usually measure the same thing; the *rate of exposure*. It is very important, however, to research the capabilities of your meter before utilizing it in an investigation. Many of the "field survey meters" or "fallout meters" available are often confused for Geiger counters, and vise versa. The difference is that most survey meters utilize an *ion chamber* rather than a Geiger-Müller detector. These meters are typically not very sensitive, and were originally designed for use only during a nuclear emergency. These meters will normally only measure high levels of gamma and high-energy x-ray radiation, and are generally useless for use in a normal environment.

This field survey meter measures in Roentgens per hour. Similar meters utilizing a Geiger-Müller tube will use mR/hr as their units and will typically measure much lower levels of radiation.

The voltage in your typical field meter ion chamber is generally very low compared to a Geiger counter, and generally only a few volts are required. Because of this there are few secondary emissions, but the resulting current is too low to accurately detect lower level radiation or individual x-ray or gamma ray interactions. Therefore these meters do not produce the individual "clicks" often associated with Geiger counters.

Secondary Emissions

A *secondary emission* occurs when a free electron impacts an electrode with enough force to free additional electrons from the surface of the electrode. Secondary emissions can occur in any electron tube, including ion tubes or GM detectors. They are more common within the GM detectors used by Geiger counters, however, because they tend to have a higher operating voltage compared to the ion chambers that are common in field meters.

Depending on the design of the meter, the presence of secondary emissions can be leveraged to provide greater sensitivity to ionizing radiation. Because a single ionization event can produce multiple free electrons, the resulting current can be more easily measured by the meter. However, this increase in secondary emissions can also produce undesirable "noise" within the chamber and skew the output of the meter. In many Geiger-Müller tubes, the purpose of adding trace amounts of other gases such as halogen is to absorb some of these secondary emissions and reduce the noise produced within the chamber. Many Geiger counters allow the user to adjust the voltage of the chamber to provide greater or lesser sensitivity to ionizing radiation.

Using a Geiger Counter

Read the Instructions

This is a very important and often overlooked (ignored) part of using a new meter.

Zero the Meter

Some meters require that the needle on the analog display be reset before use to prevent inaccurate readings. Those meters that require this usually have a fairly intuitive way of doing this. Typically this is either a button that you press to "zero" the meter or a rotary switch that you turn one way or the other to set the needle appropriately.

Some field meters I have encountered actually have a "Zero" option on the rotary switch. You would then set this switch to "Zero" and proceed to turn another rotary dial to reset the needle.

Range

Many of the Geiger counter meters I have encountered are not auto ranging, and hence have a rotary switch with several range options (similar to a lot of multimeters). The ranges include X100, X10, X1, and X0.1. These are basically pretty self explanatory. X1 means the readings on the display are correct and require no conversion, and X100 means that you'll need to multiply the readings on the display by 100 to get the correct reading.

Example range switch on a field meter is shown here. Similar options exist on many Geiger counters.

Scanning

Like most detectors, the reading on the meter will vary depending on the "strength" of the source (the amount of radiation being emitted) and the distance and proximity of the probe from the source. If the meter has a probe, hold the probe with one hand and the main unit in the other. Some meters have holsters or straps for the main unit that makes carrying them very convenient. In this case you will primarily be "listening" to the audible sounds the meter makes to determine the strength and distance of the source. Even so, it is still often a good idea to take a look at the meter on occasion and keep tabs on the baseline, even if it does not appear to change much from one location to the other.

Many probes look like round metal tubes or cylinders. These are usually end-window detectors which mean the window (the end of the tube) often needs to be pointed at or near the source to get an accurate reading. This is also true with "pancake" or paddle type detectors, although the window is typically larger.

To effectively scan an area, slowly move and "point" the sensor around an area. It is difficult to scan a room from a single location, so you will likely need to move around the room and get close to objects to effectively locate a source. A lot of different objects can contain radioactive materials. Pay close attention to antiques or charms, furniture, as well as any painted or glazed glassware. For weaker sources, it is often necessary to place the sensor very close to the object in order to detect the radiation.

Stationary Unit

It is also somewhat common to utilize a Geiger counter as a stationary unit. This is especially useful to use with meter that can store or log its data to a computer. Analysis of this data can often yield interesting information about the environment such as subtle changes in background radiation that may occur over a long period of time. Some folks have also documented a notable increase or decrease in the baseline just before or after other paranormal activity occurs. Different instruments will likely use different units of measurement, although you will likely see units such as rads/hr or roentgen(R) or milliroentgen(mR). As always, it is very important to note the exact units used when recording this data in your reports.

Motion Detectors

A motion detector is a very effective device for sensing ghostly movement. When a spirit or ghost moves past a motion detector, the movement will set off the detector just as if a living person passed in front of the device. Motion detectors can be placed in an area that is very active and when the detector sounds you know that there is activity in that area.

A motion detector can be used to trigger recording equipment. Using invisible infrared beams or vibration sensors, a motion detector can be used to remotely detect moving objects, opening doors and windows and even the appearance of hot spots. These can be used to sense movements by often unseen forces or spirits. Battery operated units sell for about 20 dollars and they are great for inside. They may also be used outdoors successfully if placed correctly so that natural occurrences do not set them off.

Night Vision Equipment

This tool may be useful in viewing some spirit activity. Many groups have reported some success with them. Some digital cameras such as the Sony Handy-cam have a function called "night shot" that provides for night vision photography. Night vision scopes can be adapted to fit video recorders or cameras, while others have a connection for direct recording. Night vision scopes can be obtained from sporting goods stores for under $300. Infra red cameras and low light cam-corders are valuable tools for the ghost hunter and are available at security shops and high end electronic shops.

Radio Frequency (RF) detectors

These devices can detect frequency that is outside the normal field of human experience. Radio frequency meters measure in the general range of 1-4500 MHz (or 4.5 GHz). This is a range of the electromagnetic spectrum used for communications and the devices can be used to check for cell phone activity, concealed bugging devices, remote cameras, etc. Sometimes paranormal phenomena have been associated with the lower range of RF signals as well as short bursts of high energy microwaves. It is known that human cells generate low RF frequencies, although there is no proven scientific explanation for why it occurs.

Spot Lights

Small battery powered spot lights really help at night when it comes to setting up and taking down cameras and other equipment. They can also be used for safety and to get a better view of the surrounding terrain at night. Use lights that sit on the ground.

Powerful spotlights such as a mariners or boaters spotlight generate half a million candlepower. This much light shows all the dust motes and particles that are floating in the air that the camera may pick up as an orb.

Static electricity and ionization detectors

Ghostly activity may ionize the air to produce negatively charged particles called ions. This phenomenon is easy to measure with an air ion counter. Static electricity and ionization emit light when the source field discharges into the air. Also, high ionization levels sometimes indicate the presence of radioactivity, and a Geiger counter survey might be indicated in such cases. Air Ion Counter: Measures positive and negative Ions in the air. This little add-on is a great instrument to have for use in the field. The price is high, around $400 - $600.

Air ion meters are capable of detecting atoms in the air that have a net positive or negative charge. These meters produce an air flow across the sensors. A current is then produced when the ions are *grounded* on the sensors. These meters tend to be more expensive ($250+).

Sound wave detectors

These devices can detect sound frequencies beyond normal human hearing, either above or below those frequencies that are normally heard.

Thermometer or Thermal Scanner

Cold spots are another manifestation the depletion of energy by paranormal events. Since cold spots are short-lived and tend to move about, conventional thermometers are not fast enough to record the phenomenon. The accepted way to check for cold spots is to use instant-reading infrared digital thermometers. It is best to add a laser pointer to these meters for good aim. Then the investigator simply has to point and shoot to get instant temperature readings of

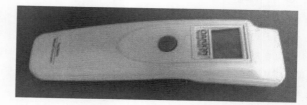

surfaces 10 to 50 or more feet away. For ambient or background temperature readings, a common thermometer or thermocouple device is sufficient.

The thermal scanner is a digital thermometer that sends out an infrared beam that bounces back when it makes contact with a surface. The instrument will then display the temperature of the surface from which the infrared beam was reflected. Before starting an investigation record the ambient temperature of the area in question. Ghostly and paranormal anomalies will cause a drop in temperature that can average between twenty and sixty degrees. When a cold spot is encountered, measure the ambient temperature outside the cold spot and compare it with the temperature inside the cold spot. In this way one can determine if cold spots are moving or if they are stationary.

A digital thermometer can be purchase for less than 50 dollars. More expensive point and shoot thermal scanners were designed for industry to obtain temperatures from a distance by focusing the instrument on a solid object and obtaining a reading. Use the thermal scanner guns in indoor areas because they shoot out a beam that reads the temperature of whatever it hits. A regular digital or analog thermometer works better out side because it is detecting the air that is currently in, so if you hold it in a cold spot and then move away, you would get a temperature increase and that would give you a truer reading of the temperature difference.

Infrared Thermometer
These units have an infrared beam that reflects off of a target. The light reflected back to the meter corresponds to the temperature of the reflecting surface.

Therefore these meters can only measure the *surface temperature*. The distance and angle of the target can have an effect on the measurement these units provide. Take a look at the documentation that comes with the meter, or is sometimes printed on the meter itself for a better understanding of the unit's capabilities.

Measuring ambient air temperature
You can use a plain old thermometer or any meter that measures the temperature of the air. It is important to know how long it takes for the unit to measure the air temperature.

A thermocouple is simply the name of the electronic component that measures temperature. These units are great at measuring ambient air temperature. There are several types and styles of thermocouple meters on the market ranging from about $75 and up. The type-T thermocouple unit is the best to use because it is slightly more sensitive than the type-K units. Like many meters, thermocouple meters typically have a sampling rate. This is usually from 1-3 samples per second. Faster is better.

Fluctuations of more than 10 degrees have been recorded in small areas of rooms with constant temperatures. In many ghost sightings witnesses report feeling a cold spot. Temperature does not change unless "something" is affecting it one way or the other. One theory states that ghosts absorb both light and heat energy causing the general area around that ghost to be several degrees cooler. There are also hot spots which could be the reverse affect occurring. Instead of soaking up the light and heat the ghost is reflecting it back, causing the area to be warmer.

Two Way Radios
These are helpful when the investigators split up and work in different areas. They allow clear communication and can eliminate searching for lost members. In large areas such as cemeteries, large facilities or battlefields they can be invaluable. Two-way radios are an easy way to keep in communication when doing an investigation in an area or building that may require members of an investigative team to split up into groups. Cell

telephones can be a life saver in the event of an emergency. Personal radios can be useful with groups spread over large areas. They can be used for responding to events or just to coordinate group activity. Some groups use headsets attached to their radios for hands free communication.

Radios

Radios can also be used to monitor the sounds from a room while no one is present to disturb the activity. Inexpensive baby room monitors are available that allow parents to "eavesdrop" on the baby room without waking the child. These can be used by ghost hunters to listen  into sounds in an attic, basement or remote location without disturbing the ghost.

Video cameras

A video camera can provide constant and continuous visual and audio surveillance. Use a tripod for best results. A regular camcorder can be used for video taping in lighted or day light conditions. The Sony line of camcorders has an infrared night-shot feature that enables you to video tape in complete darkness and sees beyond what the human eye can see.

Any video camera, analog or digital, will work for capturing anomalies on video. The best cameras are those that have night settings for filming in dark and low light situations. The camera can be carried with you or placed on a tripod and left to record in an area that is known to be an active location. Sony has developed "Nightshot" technology, which is a zero-lux infrared night vision feature. This is an excellent feature because it will record video in very low light and up to 10 feet in total darkness.

When setting up a video camera, place it in an area with an unobstructed view of the entire area that is under investigation. Be careful not to place the camera in an entry or exit and do not place it in an area where it would block the activity of other investigators. When recording begins, state the date, time, location, weather conditions and the names of the investigators participating in the event. Also state any obstruction that may be in the video that may be perceived during a review as an anomaly. Light sources or steam vents may be interpreted as something out of the ordinary by mistake, so let the reviewer know what is in the scene. The reviewer will mark down the times that a phenomenon is observed and compare it with the investigators notes.

Video recording devices should have some form of infrared recording capability. These devices are very useful for documenting interviews, investigations, and experiments. They can also help keep track of time and document your measurements.

Hi8 (8mm)
These are the less expensive units (under $350). Tapes are cheaper and can typically run for 120minutes. Transfer to a PC takes longer, unit must plug into a video card that can record directly from the camcorder.
Digital 8 (8mm)
Able to use the less expensive Hi8 media. Recording is done digitally for easier transfer to a PC via a Firewire interface.

Mini DV
Requires the more expensive MiniDV tapes, but records the data at a higher quality, and digitally for easier transfer to PC. Tapes are typically only 63 minutes. These units have the advantage of being able to easily transfer the video to a PC. It is also has the ability to record directly to a PC via USB or Firewire, and transfer other analog or NTSC video to a PC.

DVD
Can be more expensive compared to the other alternatives. Records directly to a DVD for easy viewing. Recording time depends on image quality.

Voice Recorder
A voice recorder can be used instead of a notepad to take notes. It may also pick up EVPs during an investigation (Electronic Voice Phenomenon). Not all digital recorders have a Personal Computer (USB) interface. If they don't, then you will need to download the data using the same method as you would a cassette.

Analog Audio Recorders
This is basically a cassette recorder. Micro cassette recorders are typically smaller but the tapes are also lower quality. Still useful for notes and some EVP work. Regular cassettes and recorders are inexpensive, media is low cost and easy to find, and the tapes are typically longer duration. Make sure you have a tape counter so you can indicate in your notes when events occur. To prevent false positives(eg. EVPs) only use one side of the tape. Sometimes the moving parts of the cassette recorder can cause strange sound anomalies on the recording. Therefore, you will always want to use an external microphone instead of the internal one. When the investigator is finished with the tape the tabs should be broken off to preclude the chance of recording over that tape and any evidence that may be on it.

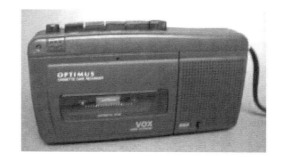

Digital Audio Recorders
Digital recorders are dropping in price, but still generally more expensive than cassette recorders. One disadvantage with digital is that once the device is full, you need to either delete the data or save that data to a PC. There are a few digital recorders out there that have removable memory cards. These are typically very expensive,

however. One major advantage to digital is that, with some devices, the audio can be downloaded to a computer and stored/analyzed more efficiently than analog meter.

Notes regarding audio patterns:

- The audible range for an average human is roughly within 20Hz to 20kHz.
- The acoustic range below 20Hz is called *infrasonic*.
- The acoustic range above 20kHz is call *ultrasonic*.
- The *voice frequency* (*VC*) or *voice band* is defined as a set of frequencies within the audible range that is used for the transmission of speech.
- The voiced speech of a typical adult male will have a *fundamental frequency* of 85Hz to 155Hz. A typical adult female will have a fundamental frequency of 165Hz to 255Hz. The fundamental frequency is defined as the lowest frequency in a *harmonic series*.
- Link: http://en.wikipedia.org/wiki/Voice_frequency

Tape recorder with an external microphone and high grade tapes are used for witness interviews, capturing spontaneous thoughts in the field as well as recording electronic voice phenomenon 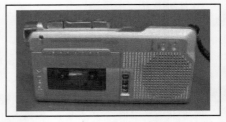 (EVP). Digital recorders are available that can record up to five hours of sound and transfer these files electronically to computers. These are available at Radio Shack and often have a voice activation feature. Most units record the time of the recording. This makes it easier to share and review EVP. If using analog tape, remember that each time you listen to the tape it will lose some of its signal strength.

Microphones

Common microphone types include *omnidirectional, bidirectional, cardioid, hypercardioid,* and *shotgun.* Depending on the design of the microphone, the unit may be more sensitive to sounds coming in from all directions (*omni-directional shown here in the photo*), sounds coming in from one direction (*unidirectional*), or sounds coming in from two specific directions (*bidirectional*). There is no "wrong" microphone to use during an investigation. Because of its versatile range, an omnidirectional microphone is typically suggested for note taking or documenting an investigation and can also work very well to capture EVPs. For now much of the basis in choosing a microphone is preference.

When purchasing microphone equipment or preamplifiers, pay close attention to what is called the *frequency response* of the microphone. This will usually be a frequency range, for example 50Hz-15kHz. Generally speaking, for our uses a wider range is better.

Condenser Microphone
A *condenser microphone*, also called a *capacitor microphone*, utilizes a membrane attached to one end of a capacitor. Fluctuations in the membrane alter the voltage maintained across the capacitor plates. Because a polarizing voltage must be maintained across the capacitor, these microphones require an external power source supplied from a battery or through the cable from the recording device.

Foil Electret Microphone
The *foil electret* microphone is a common type of condenser microphone. An electret is a dielectric material (an electric insulator) that has been permanently polarized or charged. Since the electret is permanently charged they require no external power source like a standard condenser microphone, however many of these microphones have a built-in preamplifier which do require external power.

Dynamic Microphone
A *dynamic microphone* relies on a property of electromagnetism called *induction*, which describes a phenomenon by which a changing magnetic field crossing through a conductor creates a voltage within the conductor.

The dynamic microphone utilizes a coil of wire that is suspended in a magnetic field. One end of the coil is attached to a diaphragm, which causes the coil to move when it comes in contact with vibrations in the air, such as sound waves. Movement of the coil within the magnetic field produces a current, which is then fed to a recording device.

Use an external omni-directional microphone and high bias or metal tapes when recording EVPs. Parabolic microphones amplify sounds from a distance that may be below the range of hearing.

As in video recording, start the tape with the location, time and investigators names. Since this is a sound recording, have each investigator state their names so that the reviewer can recognize their voice on the tape and not mistake a word from the investigators as a phenomenon. Voice activation modes should not be used since it normally cuts off the beginnings of words, sentences and phrases. Use the counter of the tape recorder to identify locations on the tape where audible phenomenon is heard.

EVPs are usually not heard at the time of recording but are heard only after the tape is reviewed so view or listen to the whole tape. Review notes where you should have recorded any normal sounds as well as unexplained ones (dogs barking, cars, etc.) Attempt to tell what a sound may have been that wasn't heard at the time of recording but is now on the tape.

EVP and listening devices allow investigators to actually listen to EMF energy levels and patterns, and sometimes this proves a very effective means of investigation of paranormal events. Although it is less quantitative, it provides immediate and very personal feedback. Electronic Voice Phenomena (EVP) has been picked up on just about any common recording devices from radios and tape recorders to televisions. For paranormal research, the best tool is a digital recorder that can be uploaded directly into a personal computer for analysis.

EVP is a means for recording ghostly voices on tape. Take a tape recorder and insert a tape and then start asking questions and recording. The recorder may be carried in your hand or left in a specific location. Any brand of recorder will work, and most ghost hunters use both analog and digital recorders. An important aspect of collecting EVP is to know the voices of people who might be recorded talking on the tape so you can easily identify those voices and can eliminate the voices you recognize. When talking to spirits or ghosts invite or encourage them to speak or answer by asking them questions. Investigators tend to have the most success when they speak to them as if they were alive and by interacting as if they were having regular conversations with someone standing next to them.

Watch or Timepiece
It is important that you have some way to measuring time. It is typically a good idea to indicate the time you enter and leave a room, and when an anomaly occurs. It will be useful later when all the investigators correlate their results.

Weather Meters and Monitors
These are typically meters that can measure temperature, relative humidity, dew point, barometric pressure, sometimes even wind speed. These are handy to have and can help to document the environment. Weather radios can provide data based on NOAA readings for the area. There has been speculation that tides may influence ghostly activity as well, and a marine weather radio provides information about high and low tides.

Watchers Kit
A tool box or "gang box" of handy and useful items should be available. This box should contain duct tape, fresh batteries, recording tape for tape recorders and video recorders. The box may contain

- Spare Batteries
- Compass
- Pen/Pencil/ChalkNotepad
- Graph Paper (for mapping)
- Anything else!

The Methodology

Hunting Ghosts involves applying a scientific method to something unknown. There are a wide variety of tools available to help the ghost hunter, but the right tool must be used and a system must be put in place to reach a sound conclusion. If a person were lost in the woods with a compass and a map they would have the correct tools to find their way home, but they have to know how to use them. Many hikers get hopelessly lost when they assume that they know where they are. By climbing to the top of a hill, they may be able to see Mount Ranier off to the South and Seattle's Space needle to the North East. By reading the direction from the compass, they can draw lines from these identifiable marks onto their map. Where the lines intersect is the map location of the hiker.

Ghost hunters must obtain a variety of information as well. If one person tells them that a facility is haunted, that person may be prone to exaggeration or excitement. It could be passed off as a rumor. But if another, separate person relates a similar finding about the same facility it could be speculated that there is some haunting going on there.

In military intelligence circles discussion centers around "lines of intelligence". A line of intelligence is data that is provided to a central area for processing. One line is considered chatter; two lines would be considered an indicator. If a third line is found from a separate reliable source the data becomes information that can be used.

- 1 Line = Rumor
- 2 Lines = Speculation
- 3 Lines = Confirmation

Remember that the source of these lines must be independent of each other, reliable and sound. If one person says that a castle is haunted and a second person says "yeah, I saw something there, too", the second person may be feeding on their imagination.

Recently a group conducted a visit to a cemetery in Seattle where the famous martial arts actor Bruce Lee is buried. While standing at the gravesite an investigator noticed that the compass on his binoculars was not working correctly. This could be some evidence of ghostly activity, but he did not report it to anyone in the group since this was not an investigation, but merely a "walk in the park". At the next meeting of our group, another person mentioned that she had picked up some interesting electronic voice phenomenon near Bruce Lee's grave. That would constitute a second line of independent information. At that point the group speculated that something was going on and further investigation was warranted, attempting to find that third line of information.

When conducting investigations or expeditions be aware of the mental state of those involved who are not members of the team.

Some people want to be educated or comforted about the spirits and some may want to drive the spirits away or welcome them. Be prepared to handle these people with a list of names of people who may be able to help them. Try to educate them so that they understand what is happening. Many who witness this type event lose their fear and apprehension once they understand that is occurring.

Investigation versus an Expedition
Ghost hunters are most often viewed as conducting investigations of hauntings or sightings. During an investigation a team of trained ghost hunters use their skill and equipment to validate or explore a reported haunting. The team usually has control over the area and can exclude anomalies that they may be able to control at the site.

Many organizations consider a ghost hunt and an investigation to be the same thing. As a result, they approach any ghost activity in the same manner. This redundant activity results in missed opportunities for investigation when a certain piece of equipment would be useful but was not brought to the hunt. On the other hand, sometimes these groups bring all sorts of equipment that fails to pick up any activity because there was no activity to detect.

The National Ghost Hunters Society feels that there are two separate events which are part of a series of events leading to a conclusive investigation. If an area has been documented as being haunted there is no need to hunt for ghosts. On the other hand, if an area has no reported history of a haunting a ghost hunt or expedition may be in order. At this point the hunters attempt to find any evidence that may support the theory of an active haunt taking place and the need for further investigation. Once the evidence suggests a haunting is taking place an investigation can be undertaken complete with witness statements, initial activity, what type of entity is causing the haunting and what type of events are occurring. Armed with this information the investigation team can select the appropriate equipment and staff to undertake an investigation.

Many organizations use the term Expedition as a ghost hunting term. During an expedition the group is looking for signs or evidence of ghostly activity that may or may not exist. Sometimes expeditions just turn out to be truly a walk in the park, and nothing more.

An Investigation is more detailed and more exact. When an organization conducts an investigation they have reason to suspect ghostly activity due to a report or observation. They also know a little about the activity and have an idea of what type of equipment to bring to document the activity.

The Walk Through

Most organizations conduct a walk through of a suspected haunted location prior to the arrival of the investigation team. This is done to determine what type of suspected activity is taking place and what type of equipment would best serve the investigators. During the walk through the lead group will seek evidence to support the theory that an active haunting is indeed taking place that warrants further research. The team will find out about the history of the location. One member of the team should take five or ten photographs during the walk through. Another member should develop a map showing the location of electrical appliances, fuse boxes, computers and ventilation systems that may affect the instruments of the investigation team. The team may check out the area during daylight hours so that they are familiar with the geography, looking for any dangerous obstacles or places that may not be visible in the dark. No trespassing signs must be honored and permission must be obtained from land or property owners. If in a graveyard it is a good idea to inform the local Police of the organizations activity and that they have permission to be there. If asked to leave, do so immediately. Investigators should carry their organization identification as well as government issued identification.

The walk through team advises the investigation team regarding what they can expect, but is careful NOT to inform the investigation team of the reason/type of haunting. This is done so that the investigators are not lead to a false conclusion that may affect the credibility of the investigation.

The walk through team normally consists of:
- Team lead
- Lead technician
- Interviewer
- Observer

What is an Investigation?

An investigation is researching a location that is suspected to be haunted. Observations must be objective as opposed to subjective in order to meet the scientific criteria for evaluating a haunting. Investigations are broken into five separate categories:

- Apartments
- Hotels
- Land
- Businesses
- Private homes

Ghost hunters want to know more about ghosts. Having them investigate a place of business or home will help in the pursuit of evidence. Ghost hunters work with high-tech equipment and credible psychics in a team setting that works together to seek the answers to what might be going on.

When a client contacts the organization and invites the ghost hunting team to conduct an investigation one of the officers of the group will announce the invitation to the general membership. Most organizations allow members to sign up for investigation on their web site or by email. Some investigations may be limited in number due to the size or nature of the facility. The group will rotate members into the different jobs to provide experience to all members and to develop a base of trained investigators for future investigations.

A pre-investigation team consisting of one or two leaders along with a technician will meet with the person or persons at the place of investigation. At this meeting the team will conduct a short interview of the reported activity while the technician obtains initial EMF readings and maps out the area. The person who conducts the initial interview should possess good communication skills to get the most out of an initial interview.
Initial photographs and floor plans will be obtained throughout the location, looking for orbs, ectoplasm, or anything strange that might

show up. A date for the formal investigation is decided upon with the host.

The pre-investigation team will then decide the makeup of the inspection team based on the size and location of the area under investigation. The technician will make recommendations as to the type and amount of technical equipment that will be required.

The investigation team may have six to eight members participate depending on size of the location. The team will include observers, technicians, psychics and a team leader who will orchestrate their setup of the investigation, conduct the investigation and tear down of the equipment used. The team will often use photography, sound recordings, temperature recordings, electromagnetic fluctuations, even test for trace radiation and infrared observations. Tools used by the team include a copy of the floor plan as well.

In order to maintain the objectivity of the investigation team, the leaders and the host will not provide information about the site to the team. No specific information is provided to the team so that they are not inclined to report one way or another.

If a large amount of energy or a pattern to the activity is discovered the team may ask to set up an overnight surveillance. This includes setting up S.P.E.C.T.R.E. in a room that might be having a lot of activity. While this test is being conducted infrared cameras may be placed throughout the home or business to collect more evidence.

After an investigation, the client receives a copy of the investigation summary, a certificate of investigation, and a CD of the best of photos taken at the property. The report also includes a copy of the floor plan of the facility, a copy of investigators reports and findings, any EVP's or video of any phenomena observed. A copy of the S.P.E.C.T.R.E. report, geomagnetic, solar and lunar activity and a psychic summary and recommendations is provided to the host.

Every investigator or team should keep a log of events/times - everything needs to be logged, not matter how trivial. All members and clients if possible, walk through the location. One member may map location noting: air vents, heater, electrical appliances, fuse boxes, computer, etc. Mark down the temperatures in the rooms and any EMF reading you get during this walk through. One member take 5-10 test photos during the walk through. Do not discuss the details of the case during this walk through.

Any witnesses that have not been interviewed before should be interviewed by one or two investigators and taped/videoed if it is ok with the witness. Other members should walk around the location and record any feelings or observations. Only the interviewers will know the location of events and sightings.

Investigators should not make any premature conclusions. Conclusions should be formulated by the team after all the reports, photos and tapes have been reviewed.

Reports and Logs
Each member of the investigation team must fill out the appropriate report and submit them to the team leader. The reports will be made available to other members for review and comment. Cemetery investigation field reports are normally due within one week of the investigation and should contain all the data collected by the investigators such as any events that occurred and the time that they occurred.

Procedures for an investigation
In order to sign up for an investigation, walkthrough or event the member must have no outstanding reports due. One of the officers normally selects the team leader and the team and posts it on the organizations web site. Investigators should not go to a location alone, since there are living people other than ghost hunters who tend to haunt these locations. In the event of an injury the investigator would not be able to obtain help, so two or three people should be the minimum number for any type of inspection, investigation or expedition. Record what happens as a team. Isolated peaks on meters and ghostly happenings that are not correlated mean little. But if a team records an apparition, an orb and a ghostly sound on an EVP all at the same time then the team has found something worthwhile. This can be demonstrated as

actual physical evidence as opposed to anecdotal evidence of a haunting. Investigators should keep an open mind and use a pocket tape recorder to take your notes. Equipment should be attached with a "dummy cord" that goes around the hunters neck so that if the equipment is dropped from the hands it will not break on impact with the ground. Hunters must be respectful of the locations and the dead while remaining skeptical and seeking any natural or man-made causes at the same time.

Investigation Protocol
All members of the investigating team assemble at a location away from the site to coordinate activity, establish roles and ensure that they have the correct equipment. The team leader will give a brief description of the site and what is expected of the team along with the start and stop time. Maps or drawings of the facility will be handed out to the team members, and if radio communication is being used a radio check will be performed and watches will be synchronized.

Under the guidance of the team leader the group then will proceed to the haunted location where the team leader introduces his team to the client. At this time film and tapes would be loaded into the machines. Enter the site and ask for a blessing for the duration of the investigation. Many experienced groups believe that there are evil spirits in many areas such as cemeteries. Saying a ten second prayer can provide some protection against these spirits.

EVP would be done in the background, meaning that no questions would be posed toward the spirits while clients are present.

Walk around the site to get a feel for the surrounding area. This also allows the spirits to observe the team actions and get accustomed to the team. Log in the start time and weather conditions as the team sets up stationary equipment such as tripods, cameras or motion detectors. Note any areas that may cause false readings or false positive pictures.

Each member keeps a log of events/times/activities. Even trivial sounds such as a cough or a sneeze should be logged since some other member may hear that and log it as a spirit provided event. Psychics will log events and feelings and the psychic observer will record what the psychic says and reports. Technicians will record things on their instruments and the technician observer will document the technicians' findings in their reports.

Any witnesses should be interviewed in the presence of two researchers and tape recorded if at all possible. Interviewers selected for this role should be personable and possess good communication skills. Witness questionnaires should be completed and submitted to the team leader with other reports.

All team members should have the opportunity to try everything and be in different locations. Some prefer to remain in one location while others prefer to roam around the site. The team should rotate through positions to keep all members of the crew fresh and at their peak attention.

At the conclusion of the investigation the team leader will gather the team for an on-site wrap up and after action review of the investigation. The team will provide the client with a brief overview of the findings but no conclusions should be discussed at this time. The client must understand that the findings are preliminary and that a final formal report will be provided within 30 days. At the conclusion of the event the team members will assemble outside the site and offer a closing prayer.

All reports must be turned in by each member that attended the investigation within one week. An investigation review will be held within one week of the investigation to review all the findings, photos, and video and sound recordings in order to prepare the final report for the client. All digital photos and EVP's must be provided to the team leader for archive use, preferably in digital form on a CD.

What are Expeditions?

Investigators also participate in what is known as an expedition. Expeditions can take place in cemeteries, old battle fields, schools, prisons or any other place that may be frequented by ghosts. Expeditions are a great way to refine ghost hunting skills and techniques in an informal setting. Sometimes expeditions are used to scout out a place for a future investigation. There are no participation limitations at expeditions unless the property is too small for a lot of people. When participating in an expedition the ghost hunters never know what will turn up. It is always a good idea to be prepared and to check out the area in daylight to get familiar with the area and discover any dangerous places and obstacles that may not be visible in the dark.

Make sure you are not trespassing and obey any no trespassing signs. If the expedition is on private property the team should obtain permission in writing prior to the expedition. You can get permission from many owners and/or caretakers. Notify the local police that the team will be in a grave yard "taking pictures" so that the police are aware of your presence. If asked to leave do so immediately. Investigators should always bring government issued identification such as a drivers license to identify themselves. Photos have historically been better taken in the dark, but don't let that discourage any daytime photography.

Step by step procedures for conducting an expedition:
Have everyone meet near the location and decide who will work each piece of equipment. Divide into teams if necessary. Pick a person or leader that will talk to anyone who comes in contact with the group (i.e. Police, Reporters, etc.) Do not load film or tapes yet.

Enter the site and either privately or as a group ask for blessing or protection for the duration of the hunt. Many experienced groups believe that there are evil spirits in many areas such as cemeteries and by saying a 10 second prayer you can safely go about your business without worrying about them. An experienced demonologist will tell you that by doing this in the name of God or whatever good deity you worship may keep any non human spirits at bay.

Walk around the area for about 20 minutes to get a feel for the surroundings. Record the start time and weather conditions as well as any other relevant information. Set up any stationary equipment like camera on tripods or motion detectors. Make note of any areas that may cause false readings or false positive pictures.

Next, open all your film and tapes and load the cameras and recorders. Be sure to note anything unusual that happens especially meter and temperature readings, visual sightings and strange sounds. Record any feelings or emotions you feel that may be odd or out of place. You can compare notes after the hunt and look for similarities in readings and feeling in certain areas or at certain times.

The team leader should give everyone the opportunity to try everything and be everywhere. This keeps every one fresh and at attention. Rotate a few times during the investigation.

When the expedition is over have everyone meet in one spot and ask the human spirits to remain at the location. Tell the others they must remain here in the name of God (or other good deities as appropriate).

Procedures for expeditions

Procedures for expeditions are similar to those of investigations. However, they are not as formal as investigations. The same rules of evidence and investigation such as no smoking, watch out for camera straps and long hair in photos, awareness of sources of light or reflections all apply. The group gathers at a location and instead of having teams set out to investigate specific reported events, individuals select their own method of chasing ghosts. Some may want to try their hand at capturing EVP with a tape recorder, while others may practice with photography or fine tune their psychic skills. Technicians may take advantage of the expedition to familiarize themselves or practice with their equipment.

The group gathers at the appointed place and the expedition leader (who has obtained permission from the owner) provides a brief summary of the location and any reported hauntings. The leader establishes a start and stop time and often says a welcome prayer and invites the spirits to show themselves. The group spends a few hours exploring the area and then meets back at a central location where the leader says a closing prayer and members conduct a brief after action review of what they found and any lessons learned during the expedition.

After the expedition each member must fill in an expedition report form and submit it to the organization through the team leader. During the next meeting of the organization the team leader provides a public summary of the group's activity. Any EVP or photographs should be shown at the group meeting.

Lake View Cemetery Expedition
(Case Study)

The purpose of this expedition was to acquaint members with a Seattle cemetery where the remains of some of the founding families (the Denny family, the Mercers, the Yeslers) of Seattle are buried. Quite often cemeteries demonstrate the lives of those founders of a city or region in the artwork and carvings that go into the

memorials that are left behind. The club historian presented a field trip class on Iconography, the study of engravings and stonework found in graveyards. The group met at the front of the cemetery near the statue shown at the right.

Since this was an expedition as opposed to an investigation the team leader was only responsible for conducting initial and ending accountability of the group members. These members generally stayed together as a group and learned quite a bit from the historian. Some members wandered away to use equipment that they had brought with them such as tape recorders, cameras and compasses. There was no coordinated effort to investigate any particular reported sighting. The event truly was a "walk in the park." Most participants enjoyed learning about the cemetery and some of the unique grave markers there.

Beautiful stone works adorned the cemetery and provided a glimpse into the lives of people who had been dead for several decades. Their love of children, teaching and nature was displayed in the monuments that adorned their final resting place. Some mysteries of a historical nature were discussed, such as the gravestone that had a piano carved on it with one key missing. *Was that key deliberately left out to leave a clue about the person interred, or was the key removed by vandals. And why just that one key?*

At the next bi-weekly meeting of the ghost hunter group the members stood and presented an oral repot on their findings.
Mysterious sounds were recorded on tape by one member while another member reported erratic

behavior of a compass, both events occurring near the grave of Bruce Lee. This was the first time that these separate events had been reported among the group.

Based on the information presented at the meeting a more formal investigation may be warranted at a future date. Such an investigation would most likely center on the activity identified during this expedition and members would bring technical equipment, observers, technicians and psychics to record their findings in a more structured manner.

The Des Moines Marina Park Expedition

Prior to the expedition the group was aware that the park was the scene of an annual haunting on January 8. It seems that a little girl was seen on the park near the beach and later moved to the swing set. The previous year the group had conducted an expedition with some anecdotal success that indicated that additional

study was truly warranted. This was the limited information that was available to the group at the start of this expedition. The park closes at dusk, so the vice president of the group got permission from the city to occupy the park in the evening.

During the expedition

Psychics expected to pick up the impression of a little girl. During the four hour expedition they picked up the impressions of lots of children as well as an old man who the children referred to as a camp grounds keeper. Discussion with observers at the site revealed that there was a rumor that the park had at one time been a Christian campground.

When the psychics felt a presence, the president of the group would direct that the other members take photographs of the area indicated. Psychics also felt the presence of an old man who did not seem to want the investigators around.

One area of the grounds had an outbuilding on it, sort of a storage building. The building had been visited by the psychic who got a strong impression that the entity inside the building did not want the investigators near and that they should go away. Another researcher attempted to get video of the inside of the building, but the power on the camcorder always failed....

A group of onlookers reported seeing a little girl in a white dress go up the hill. A team from the group compromised of a psychic and a technician went up the hill to investigate.

The technician took blind photographs (nothing was visible to the naked eye) and the psychic tried to gain any impressions that she could. The psychic did pick up the impression of a little girl.

Above photo shows something in the distance, perhaps the spirit that the onlookers reported. A close up and enhanced image of the same thing is on the left. Is this a spirit, or merely a reflection? The image below is a daytime picture of the same area.

The Des Moines Beach Park was the founding place of the current city of Des Moines. The pathway above the trees was the road that linked this town with the city of Seattle. Now the park is a National Historic area that is enjoyed by children and the community every day. And perhaps some of the previous visitors still show up from time to time.

Several lumber mills were built alongside Des Moines Creek before the turn of the century. An historic photograph shows a mill of uncertain ownership being consumed in a spectacular, smoky fire. In 1917 or 18 a Mr. Draper had a Children's Home just above the Des Moines Creek ravine and sought beach access and a place for the children to play. He built rustic cabins for public rental and added a rudimentary playground and a small kitchen for picnickers. The Draper family rented cabins to summer visitors until 1934 when they sold the property to the Covenant (Swedish Baptist) Church.

Information obtained at the Des Moines Public Library from the Des Moines Beach Park- Final Master Plan Executive Summary. The Partico Group- Architects, 1916 Pike Place, Room 221, Seattle, WA 98107, 11 June, 1987.

Those old familiar places have ghosts!

Just like any social group, ghosts tend to hang around certain areas. Such places as a location where a violent or mysterious death has occurred seems to be ripe for ghostly investigations. Some places to check out would be a battlefield or a place where a mass murder was committed, or even an area where an accident occurred, such as a road intersection or factory that burned down with a loss of life.

Cemeteries and graveyards are popular places to find phantoms and apparitions that have been rumored to occur. For some reason churches have some of the most popular ghostly events around. Such events as bells ringing, candles lighting and moving on their own and glowing lights inside the empty church have been reported.

Old buildings that are more than a hundred years old tend to harbor ghosts, so check out the older hotels and public buildings in the area and ask about any ghostly happenings. Colleges and schools often have a ghost story to investigate as well. Ghosts have been known to float across campus and be seen from dorm room windows.

Theaters are another likely place to find spirits who may be the ghosts of actors, employees or patrons of the past. Current tenants often avoid a certain balcony or dressing room due to spooky feelings or strange occurrences.

Prisons and other old institutions such as Alcatraz have been reported to house spirits that refuse to move on. Concentration camps, slave camps and old military prisons seem to have a lot of ghostly events associated with the institution where people were forced to remain together, usually in painful situations.

Below is a listing of some "haunted" locations in Washington. *Some of these locations are privately owned while others are located on Federal, State or County lands. Get consent from the owner before conducting an investigation. Ghost hunters should inform the local police of their activities in the event someone reports suspicious activity.*

Aberdeen- The first floor of Billy's Bar and Grill houses a restaurant, while the second floor used to contain a house of prostitution. Some of the ladies and a very infamous ghost named Billy Ghol are said to haunt the place. Lights go on and off at night, cold spots are abundant and fog forms on the plate glass mirror.

Auburn- At the Cinema 17 Super Mall Theater a spirit is reported to be found in the projection area. Movies turn off by themselves in theaters 2, 9, and 17 for no apparent reason.

At the Fred Meyer Shoe Store employees and customers have reported shoes being thrown at them and the sound of boxes being moved around when no one is there and there is no mess. On occasion employees and even customers have reported having shoes thrown at them.

Auburn High School Auditorium - A young girl has been sighted wandering around the pit area and in the cat walk. It has been reported that a girl fell from the catwalk during a production in the 1950's.

Arlington - Old Arlington High School - A maintenance worker fell from the roof of the auditorium and broke his neck on the back of one of the chairs. He has been reported walking at night on the top floor of the school and in the auditorium. A cheerleader has also been reported to be seen stalking the halls. Rumors of a "lost room" underneath the high school may be an old bomb shelter.

Eagle Creek - Sometimes Indians can be seen next to the creek and in a mobile home park. One trail is known to confuse people who get lost ending up miles from where they thought they were.

In the upstairs floor of the condemned gym building of the old Presidents Elementary school it has been reported that you can see a class walking up there wearing older fashioned clothing.

Bellingham- At "The Mansion" a man pacing and a woman screaming in pain are heard here, where a woman had died in childbirth.

At the Old Town Café located in the "Overland Block" piano music has been reported, although there is no piano inside.

Employees also reported observing dishes float for 15 minutes, then return to their original place. The building was built in the 1890's.

The Mount Baker Theatre has a ghostly woman that seems to want nothing more then to watch over her property and its present owners.

In the Shuksan Rehab Center rooms have moving objects, call lights go on and off by themselves, and you can hear someone walking with a walker in middle of night. Two registered nurses saw ghosts in the hallway, walking through the door. The building was built on a lot where an old school existed from the1800s into the 1950s.

Black Diamond- In the Black Diamond Cemetery one can see the swinging lights of a coal miner's lantern. People can also sometimes hear whistling in the wind, supposedly that of the coal miners. It is reported that a white horse has sometimes been seen trotting around headstones.

Bremerton – The Chester Apartments was once a hospital and ghostly patients and orderlies have been reported roaming the halls.

Burien- Years ago a young boy hung himself at the Lakeside Milam Treatment Center and has been seen by employees wandering the halls.

Carnation – At the Carnation Cemetery witnesses report hearing footsteps, whispers and seeing figures in the corners of their eyes. A woman in a white dress has been reported numerous times in the company of a boy.

Fall City/Carnation Back Road - Reports of a white ghostly looking dog. Witnesses claim to accelerate and drive three miles down the road where they find the dog sitting and watching them at the new location.

Concrete - Mount Baker Hotel – Visitors to the Mount Baker Hotel should prepare themselves to go upstairs to see a little girl about four years old with red hair and blue jean shorts on and a pink shirt on. She has been reported to try to push visitors down the stairs but it does not work. All they feel is a sort of tingle go through your body.

The little girls voice can be heard saying "The bad woman's gonna hurt me!" Visitors also report hearing "Turn around; the bad woman will hurt you!" Rumor has it that her mother beat her to death.

Coupeville – At the Sunnyside Cemetery near Ebey's Landing a headless ghost has been reported in the cemetery and in an old cabin his family occupied after his death.

The old one room schoolhouse is now used as a rental unit where the ghost of a small girl dressed in period clothing is well known to long-time locals. Some have reported seeing the ghost while driving by the schoolhouse when she is seen looking out the window or on the front porch of the old school.

Des Moines -The Des Moines Marina Park at 22030 Cliff Ave S is the birthplace of the city. The ghost of a little girl named Diana has been reported walking the beach and swinging on the swing set at the beach park at night every January 8th. (Bear in mind that this city park is closed from dusk to dawn)

Edmonds- The Frances Anderson Leisure and Cultural Arts Center was built in 1929 ad is haunted. It was named after Frances Anderson, a longtime teacher and principal for the school. The original structure was called Edmonds Elementary School and is now owned and operated by the Edmonds Parks and Recreation Department. Employees and visitors have reported haunting activity for years that involve spirits of children walking the hallways as well as the ghost of Frances Anderson herself, who died in the 1980s.

Ellensburg- Ellensburg was competing to become the capital of the state in that late 1890's. It was also the site of some gruesome crimes that were committed by a man named Greg who lived in a building that once stood at 206 East Tacoma Street. It is said that Greg was the offspring of a brother and sister who got married and were Satanists. Greg grew up under their influence and one day began to kidnap local children for use in ritual sacrifices. The towns' people formed a lynch mob but before they got to Tacoma Street Greg killed himself and set his house on fire. The flying embers ignited the rest of the buildings in Ellensburg, burning most of the city to the ground on July 4, 1898. With little of Ellensburg left standing, the city of Olympia became the state capital. The story of Inbred Greg continues to be discussed on the 200 block of East Tacoma which now houses the U-Haul dealership and Play and Pack and Independent Auto shops. People have reported encounters with a bearded Greg complete with thick glasses, body odor and stinky feet. The manager of U-Haul may share the spooky story with visitors and has been known to hold séances and sometimes a full moon sleep over.

Kamola Hall at Central Washington University is haunted by the ghost of a former student that committed suicide when she found out that her fiancé had been killed during the war. She hung herself from the rafters of the top floor where her room was located. People have reported unusual noises and sightings over the years. Some of the current students residing in the building have reported strange occurrences such as doors opening and closing and doors being knocked on by ghosts.

Everett- It is reported that when the Everett High School Auditorium was being built a construction worker fell and was killed. Many people have seen his ghost in the school and on the grounds.

The old Everett Movie Theatre is located in downtown of north Everett. Several people have seen an apparition or ghost in the theatre over the last 20 years. The ghost is believed to be male, either an old deceased patron or worker of the theatre. Psychics have been called in and have reported a supernatural presence.

Around midnight at the Mariner High School the lights are supposed to be on like a normal school. Yet, on some nights, the lights shut off and if you're close enough, you can see and sense eyes staring at you from within the school. Nothing can be seen but the eyes, which look like floating eyes from a distance. It is too dark to see the body, but you can see the eyes because they have a subtle glow to it. It has been reported that if you stare at them for a while you can see a figure of a winged man.

Fairhaven-
According to legend, three Spanish war ships landed on the shores of what is now Fairhaven and began to construct a fort by creating a "mound" above high tide with a deep channel around it. The mound

was separated by water at all times and could only be approached by boat and the Spaniards began to build a fort called Ma-Mo-Sea on the mound. The Native Americans felt threatened and called on several neighboring tribes to join them in a midnight attack. The violent battle resulted with many lives lost, the ships were gone and not a living Spaniard remained.

The Ghosts of Fairhaven are quite active in town today. Almost every building lay claim to a ghost - Dos Padres has a very active one, as well as one in the Doggie Diner building. Hangings regularly fall off the walls, and the staff often finds open file drawer cabinets in the office upstairs. Apparently this was once the office space of the resident ghost - and she visits on occasion to work on her unfinished projects.

The Morgan Block (which currently houses Good Earth Pottery) served as a viewing area for the "Unclaimed Dead" as late as the 1900's. During the 1890's and 1900's thousands of transients came to help build the "New City of Fairhaven." Some died of exposure, some by accident and some committed suicide. When the bodies could not be identified, they were loaded into a wagon and put on display in hopes that someone would identify them.

The Bellingham Bay Hotel at 907 & 909 Harris Avenue was built in 1901 and housed a busy brothel in the red light district of Fairhaven. Decent women did not venture unescorted below 9th Street because of the bordellos and saloons. Current shop owners at Fairhaven Hardware, Nature's Window as well as in the new Drummond Building have reported thumping sounds, store music going on and off and footsteps in the hall.

Finnegan's Alley is just down the street a few blocks on 1114 Harris Avenue. Current and former owners of The Fairhaven Pub site don't hesitate to talk about the resident ghost, seen by a DJ, and visited often since. As he was closing up "it" appeared as a blurred reflection in a glass door. As he stared it disappeared. The current manager also reported receiving a gentle hug one day, and as recently as Sept. 2002, she was talking with a plumber in the middle of the club, when the TV came on all by itself. They stood shocked, talked about the ghost and the TV turned itself off.

At the Southeast corner of Harris and 11th street is the Nelson Block (1900).

This corner building served as a bank for over 30 years. Rumors persist of a sound of someone walking on glass at night in the upper levels. It is said a 17 year-old woman died in a dentist chair there and continues to walk the halls. In the 1970s a human skeleton was found buried in the basement as the building was being renovated. Former restaurant employees in that space reported many disturbances such as frigid air and strange noises after dark.

The Red Bus at the corner of Harris Ave & 11th S street. Unknown footsteps and creaking doors are commonplace to the workers at Jacci's Fish & Chips inside the 1948 English double-decker bus. Since their 1999 opening employees have heard strange noises both upstairs and down while working alone. Jacci herself was greeted one morning by a formerly broken stereo playing music. Some speculate the supernatural noises originate from the 50-year old bus itself, but knowing nothing of its British history we can't speculate. However, the spot where the bus now stands was home to the Town Marshal's office in the 1890's. Marshal Parker had left after one year in office for Buenos Aires with the city treasury. Perhaps he is now trapped here to pay his eternal penance.

The Quinby Bldg is located at 1007 Harris. In the year 2000, employees of the Doggie Diner were frightened by the sounds of drawers opening and closing in the empty office upstairs. When employees investigated the event an office chair rolled toward them. A computer typed things over and over. In the shop, shelves fell from walls and pictures and wall decorations flew nightly from one wall to an opposite floor. A clock fell on an employee's head. The manager reported a tug on her pony tail, someone saying "good morning" and nearly all staff heard babies crying. No one wanted to work after dark. When the owner finally sold the business, she was required to disclose the ghosts in the real estate listing. This spot was "Benton's Bath Parlor & Tonsorial Palace". Some wonder if surgery is still taking place.

Every December, a "ghost train" is rumored to run between Fairhaven, through Happy Valley and down to the Skagit. The whistle blows, the wind blasts through and the roar of the train is rumored to be heard. On December 21, 1892 a freight train pulled out of Fairhaven southbound. Earlier, a train of logs had crossed the bridge across the Skagit, and the weight of it had broken the chord above the long wooden span and sprung the bent below. The watchman had discovered the break, and a carpenter's gang had been sent up from below Mt. Vernon to make repairs. The superintendent declared it safe for passage, much to the distress of the foreman. The bridge might be safe in two hours time, but the "super" insisted the train make the crossing. As it made its way across, the bridge broke and the train tumbled into the river, killing all three men on board. Every anniversary of the crash, the ghost train runs. It runs over the same line, on a ghost track that hasn't been there for many years. It stops at stations that are but a memory, crashes and clatters on to the Skagit at the wrecked bridge, and the locomotive drops to the bottom of the river, the end of the run...

Fort Lewis is located South of Tacoma. At night, sightings of ghost apparitions are seen in the woods on North Fort Lewis. A few people say they have seen mysterious cloaked spirits as well as spirits of Native Americans.

North Fort Old Barracks - A former housekeeper reports, doors slamming & cleaning carts moving on their own.

North Fort Lewis - The cadences of platoons of soldiers running is often heard early in the morning, long before any unit of this size is conducting runs. Soldiers look outside to see who it is, and no one is there.

Friday Harbor- Roche Harbor Resort: The Mausoleum by the cemetery in Roche Harbor. There are stories that late at night on a full moon you can walk up the long trail that leads to the mausoleum, and once you arrive you can see the six people that are buried under the seats around the table, sitting there laughing and talking. It is also reputed that when it is raining you can sit at the table, and even though there is an opening in the roof of the mausoleum no rain will come in.

Index- At the Bush House Country Inn that was built in 1889 for miners coming into the area, many people have claimed to see the apparition of "Alice" or "Annabel". This young woman hanged herself at the turn of the century when she heard that her lover was killed in a mining accident. As it turned out her lover had not died but returned home to find her dead. She hung herself in room 9 and table 2 is her table, as her ghost still haunts the Bush House along with some others who have died there.

Kent- A man committed suicide by hanging himself in a stairwell at East Hill Elementary School. Students and staff have seen an apparition of a man hanging there and have reported hearing him moan and choking, while some children say that they can hear him whispering. Some people report that when they are walking near the stairs they feel a chill and their throats constrict.

Kenmore

At St. Edwards State Park (14445 Juanita Drive NE, Kenmore - Bastyr University) colds spots, moving chandeliers and things move on their own around the chalkboards and chairs in the basement. Spectral children have been reported running around in the playground at the park

Kirkland- Several residents have reported seeing a man in a hat and heard footsteps in the Williams/Web building which is now a hotel and restaurant. Some have seen objects move on their own. Workers in the restaurant have seen a shadowy figure.

Employees at the Central Tavern have reported seeing a "pink lady" near the back of the room.

Lake Stevens- A woman died in Lake Stevens Lake here when she drove through a railing into Lake Stevens. People have claimed to see her floating above the water, staring at people as they drive by.

Long Beach - The Lamplighter Restaurant had a ghost inhabiting the bar area who would play pool (while others were trying to have a game, of course) and do various other obnoxious things such as turning lights off and on. The owner of the lamplighter restaurant in long beach and the manager would like to let you know that the ashes of the deceased owner (Louie) are still on the mantle and that there are still a lot of strange things going on here.

Longview- At the Monticello Middle School there is a legend that a young girl who had taken cookies to the workers died on the site while this school was being built. She was victim to a terrible fate one day when she fell in an area of freshly poured cement. Her ghost has been seen wandering the halls of the school at night, humming a tune. The girl's footsteps have been heard as well.

At Heron Point some people have reported seeing Indians walking the streets at night on this old Indian burial ground. A tall man dressed black with a black hood has been seen in the back of the park and he seems to enjoy frightening people by sneaking behind them and whispering, then disappearing when they turn around.

Marysville- Marysville-Pilchuck Road is on the Tulalip Indian reservation. This road begins with an uphill drive and is many miles long until it ends at a dead end. Motorists have seen someone running next to their vehicles, keeping pace while looking in their windows as they drive 35 to 40 mph up the steep hill. Indians have also been seen standing on the side of the road, but when the motorists look in the rearview mirror after they have passed, no one is seen. Some say they have seen people sitting in their backseat in the rearview mirror, and turn to look but no one is there.

State Street - A dog by the name of Bud got sick one day and his owner got a gun and put him out of his misery. They say if you say his name late at night a little girl appears, and says "don't hurt him he is my dog go away." she stares at you and walks away.

Moses Lake - Columbia Basin Alternative High School - This haunting has been described as mysterious noises that happen around 11:30 P.M. An alarm has also been heard. A smoke-like apparition with only the legs showing is seen running down the hallway. Frontier Middle School - On the date of February 6, 1996, the way of life in Frontier Middle School was shattered forever when a student by the name of Barry Loukaitis stepped into his Algebra class with a high powered hunting rifle and opened fire on the students. Since that time, both students and teachers claim they can still hear the echo of gunshots and the screams of the students from that part of the building, and many students attest to a feeling of panic whenever they are in or around that area.

Moses Lake High School - In the theatre the curtains sway when no one is there. The lights turn on when there is no one there. There is a cat walk above the seats where they can be heard swaying when the door to the stairway is locked tight, and the stairs creak also when the door is locked tight. People claim that in the costume room people can feel the atmospheric imprint of people there.

The White homestead is a house that was built in 1903 and according to actual witnesses, there has been a murder that took place in that house and the ghost of the young lady with child that was murdered is still there. They have since moved the house off of its foundation, down the block and started renovating it. The workers that have been there still hear the faint screaming of a young woman.

McChord Air Force Base: A C-141 transport aircraft that was assigned to this base was used to transport bodies back from Jonestown, Guyana; South America after Jim Jones had ordered their suicides. Maintenance personnel report hearing voices and footsteps. The auxiliary power goes on and off when no one is around.

The Tribal Administration Office is in a building that was an old hospital. Noises of someone walking can be heard throughout the building. It is said that many people died of tuberculosis there and their bodies were incinerated in the incinerator in the basement. The basement also housed the morgue and a woman can be heard complaining of being cold. The fifth floor is known to be the most spiritually active floor where one can hear a woman cry for her child and/or husband. Elevators move from floor to floor on their own. Children's voices can be heard.

Olalla/Port Orchard – In the 1900's Dr. Linda Burfield Hazzard ran a sanitarium in here. She felt that any disease could be cured by a method of fasting. It is said that she intentionally starved her patients to death and buried them on the sanitarium grounds, planting a tree over each body. When she ran out of room for the bodies she threw them off the cliff on the backside of where the building once stood. (In fact, she had wills drawn up that gave her full possession of her deceased patients' money and valuables, which may account for some of the deaths.) The foundation of the sanitarium and the incinerator in which she may have cremated some bodies remains today. The trees serve as headstones to the many nameless victims of Dr. Hazzard and remain a monument to "Starvation Heights".

Orcas Island- At the Rosario Resort long-time workers for the resort have seen the deceased wife of the man who originally owned the site before it became a resort. She is commonly seen on the 2nd or 3rd floor wearing a red dress of the 1930s and driving through the 2nd floor on her old favorite motorcycle.

Oysterville- School House: The Oysterville Schoolhouse was built in the early 1900's on the Long Beach peninsula. It is said to be haunted by a child who died from an epileptic seizure.

Paradise Valley- Paradise Valley Cemetery (a.k.a. Maltby Cemetery): This cemetery is hidden off the side of Redmond/Duvall road, and has about 15 grave sites. Strange, unexplained things have been said to have happened there. People have seen women and children, dressed in old, raggedy looking clothes, wandering around the gravesites.

Port Townsend- Port Townsend is one of Washington's oldest cities and is well known for its ghosts and other mysteries. Sea serpents add to the mystery and were sited off the coast of this city in 1891 and again in 1904. The historical society promotes a Victorian Festival Cemetery Tour among other living history tours. Tours are available both on land and on water to explore these mysteries.

In May of 1899 the newspaper ran a story about the dark alleyway behind the offices of the ship brokers Rothschild and Company. This disreputable waterfront alley leads to the slips where the docks tied up. The paper reports, "Captain William Breeze, a pioneer shipmaster on the Puget Sound, claims to have encountered the ghost on several occasions during the dark hours of the night when passing through the alley.

"According to Capt. Breeze's statement, the ghost is that of a Chinese with his head split in the center. It appears in the alleyway between the hours of 12 and 1 o'clock. The first appearance of the ghost with its ghastly wound caused a thrill of terror to creep through the nervous system of the captain, and he lost no time in making a hasty retreat. Since then he has made several attempts to capture it and has succeeded in getting within reaching distance. When he would attempt to lay his hands on the wraith, it would disappear."

This same ghost was also seen by Night Inspector Bropoy of the customs service. "On making his nightly rounds in search of opium smugglers, he has encountered the tomahawked Chinese ghost. Chinese never frequent this alley, as a tradition exists among them that many years ago a Chinaman was murdered there....and his body was thrown into the bay."

Holly Hill House is a popular bed and breakfast that seems to be haunted by one or two of its former residents. Its previous owners have reported seeing a strange looking man dressed in turn-of-the-century clothing. They have also claimed to hear a piano being played, even though there is no piano in the house. Cigar smoke is often smelled in one of the upstairs bedrooms.

The Palace Hotel is a lovely hotel on the main street of Port Townsend. If you ask if they have any ghost stories, the front office manager will show you the file that has been kept for years with details of ghostly occurrences. As recently as June, 2005 a visitor walking down the main stairway felt "something brush against the back of my neck" and when photographs were taken they revealed the presence of orbs in that area.

During the winter months of 2004 a clerk was working at the Palace hotel when a guest came back late in the evening. The woman went upstairs, and then returned shortly to tell the deck clerk how nice it was of the hotel to have people to greet the guests in the hallway dressed in period costumes. Since the clerk was working alone that night, she asked what type of costume was being worn, suspecting an intruder. The guest explained that the woman that she encountered in the hallway was dressed in clothing like that of the life sized painting in the hallway. The clerk smiled and explained to the guest that she must have just met the hotels resident ghosts. At that, the guest immediately left the hotel in the middle of the night to find other, less haunted lodging.

Manresa Castle was built in 1892 with over 30 rooms. It was built by Charles Eisenbeis who was the towns' first mayor. The September 30, 1897 Port Townsend Newspaper carried a dreadful headline "SHOCKING DEATH". Charles Eisenbeis Jr. had been found dead the night before in the basement of the Baker Block family store. This spectacular hotel has been featured on the TV program "Sightings" and is open to the public who can stay and conduct their own ghost investigations and enjoy a wonderful Sunday Brunch.

The building was purchased by the Jesuit priests n 1928 who named the building Manresa Hall and used it as a training college. Legend has it that a monk who resided there committed suicide and that you can hear the rope swinging with his body some nights. It has also been reported that during the early 1900's a young girl named Kate was staying in room #306 of the castle when she heard that her fiancé had been lost at sea. She committed suicide by jumping from the third floor. There is supposed to be a portrait of Kate hanging in the lounge. One visitor took a picture and said that there was an image of a woman clothed in turn of the century attire and a bonnet staring out the window towards the ocean. While these events cannot be corroborated and another legend has it that a bartender working at the hotel made up these stories to fascinate and entertain the patrons. That story, too, has not been corroborated and it may be that the bartender story is another unfounded legend.

Today ghostly reports of singing that can be heard at night and a broken clock which chimes from time to time has been heard by the desk clerk. The clock has not worked for years. Lights go off and on by themselves and doors open and close. A book was once left in her room so that guests could record their experiences, but was removed because it scared the guests. Recently, an employee reported that when she was alone in a room a gook flew off the shelves as if tossed across the room by an unseen hand. Ghost hunters have found sufficient anomalies in the hotel to warrant further investigation.

The Rothschild house was built in 1868 on the bluff overlooking Port Townsend Bay at Taylor and Franklin Streets. It is now a State heritage site. Temperature variations and doors that slam closed by themselves have been reported.

The Bead Shop is located at the 900 block of Water Street in the Victorian style James and Hastings Building that was built in 1889. The ground floor and mezzanine are retail shops; there is a large basement and residential units above. The spacious lobby opens to the shops that include the bead store, a yarn shop and a wine merchant. The ghostly prankster in the shop made his presence known in March of 2003 and seems to enjoy frightening the shop owners and is especially fond of the female clerks. The spirit also seems to be attracted to red items for some reason. Activity tends to take place in the late evening when the building is quiet in the retail areas and the basement. Windows that are closed are found to be open, while windows that were left open are later found to be closed. Merchandise moves from one display area to be found in another area, tossed about and disordered. Skeins of yarn have been tossed over the railings and unrolled.

The proprietor was working late one evening, alone in the building and a chain barrier had been set up across a restricted space. Lois heard the sound of chains being moved and went to investigate. All was in order and no one was about. She returned to her work to hear the noise again, then the unmistakable sound of the chain being loudly handled or dropped with the metal links clinking loudly against one another. She checked the barrier and once again found herself alone in a building, which she left shortly afterward and prefers not to work late into the evening any longer.

The spirit seems to enjoy moving things and the staff was looking unsuccessfully for an advertising banner one day. After a strenuous search turned up nothing, a clerk went to the basement one last time only to find the banner neatly folded and placed in plain sight on a table by the stairs. The staff was certain that the banner had not been there moments before.

One day when Lois was closing the basement door she held the door knob in her hand and the knob was pulled out of her hand by an unseen force. The door then slammed shut.

An apparition of a man about 50 years old has been seen around the shop. He is seen wearing old fashioned clothing with a white shirt and a black string tie. He was once seen standing at a top floor window in the building which was uninhabited and unused at the time. The man disappears when his presence is investigated.

A house on Lincoln Street, near Lizzies's Bed and Breakfast was built in the early 1900's. A family living there from 1986 to 1991 would hear bumps and thumps coming from the attic. When they investigated they found that items had been shoved around when no one was in the attic. At other times they would hear low, muffled voices of people talking when no one was present. Within a few weeks of moving into the house their young son mentioned a "boy" that he was playing with. The son would speak with and play with the playmate that was invisible to the parents. This continued for six months.

Near Jolie Way, Katie Y, a resident of Port Townsend was walking outside along the dirt road near her house. She felt a tingling sensation and felt the air around her get colder that it had a moment before. She used her flashlight to look around, sensing that someone was watching her. She could find no people or cars in the area. Then, a light appeared before her about 30 feet away. Katy was frozen with surprise as she watched the light bob up and down as if someone were walking very slowly or hobbling along the road holding a lantern. She ran a bit up the street, stopped and looked back to find that the mysterious light had vanished as quickly as it had appeared. When she explained this event to her mother she mentioned that she had a mental impression of an old man in his 70's or 80's. Her mother informed her that an elderly man had once lived alone in a rustic shack on some wooded land nearby. The man died of a heart attack in 1994 but his body was not discovered until a neighbor stopped by a month later.

A house on the 1900 block of Holcomb Street was built in 1879. When new residents moved in they cleaned the dirt floor area below the washer and dryer by raking the soil beneath the deck that the machines stood on. One day the husband asked his wife why she had put a dish on the dirt floor. She didn't know what he was talking about and investigated, to find a clear bowl with water in it sitting in the center of the dirt floor. Although they did not have a cat, it seemed to be the kind of bowl one would set out for a cat. There were no paw prints or footprints in the dirt and the bowl was not one that they owned or had ever seen. This occurred when the doors were locked and no one could gain entrance.

Animals in the house have been known to behave strangely, barking into space as if they see something. The animals then look at their owners as if to say "Can't you see what I'm barking at?"

One summer afternoon the wife was walking in an upstairs hallway and felt a cool breeze and saw a brief shadow go past. This may be the same spirit that left the toilet seat up in the guest bedroom when the wife was the only one in the house and had put the seat down earlier in the day. She accused her husband of coming home during the day, but she was in the house all alone that day.

The ghosts seem to be delightfully friendly and the family living there enjoys their presence. Others have commented on the nice feeling that the house has to it and the spirits even seem to enjoy the husbands' music, humming the tunes after the band has finished practicing for the evening. Love may endure in this home for the past century and for centuries to come!

At the Laurel Grove Cemetery workers had been clearing some berry bushes from a grave site that kept people from reading the head stone. Louise F. used a rubber mat to kneel on as she worked and when she finished clearing the bushes the mat was about ten feet from her and her truck. As he tossed the last remnants of prunings into the truck she noticed that the mat was floating a foot off the ground with a little whirl-wind beneath it. The mat then shot about 20 feet into the air and returned to earth. Louise took that as acknowledgement for her labors over the neglected grave and said "You're Welcome!" to the spirits.

Another time she was cutting a shrub over a marker and was working with a pair of work gloves with large, flared cuffs. She threw the gloves to the ground to work on her task and when she looked at them again they were in an upright position beside the grave as if they were praying. Louis checked the headstone to find that it was the final resting place of a reverend.

In 2004 while working on some ivy near Enoch Fowlers gravestone, she had a feeling that she should dig deeper, pulling up roots as she went. Perhaps she was inspired by Fowlers deceased wife. After digging on the ivy and pulling up roots, she found the gravestone of Mary Caines Fowler buried eight inches below the soil. Mary Caines Fowler was a pioneer of the region in 1853 and Louise greeted the discovery of her long lost headstone by saying "Welcome back, Mrs. Fowler!"

Port Townsend Area -Fort Worden

Fort Worden overlooks Port Townsend and is currently a campsite and hostel as well as a conference center. Fort Worden is currently a campsite and hostels as well as a conference center run by the state which acquired it from the Federal Government. The fort has a rich military history and is in excellent condition.

The Post Military Cemetery is located down the road from the guardhouse/information center at the edge of the fort property. Go past the blimp hangar on the left and the campgrounds on the right. The cemetery is at the end of the road on the left. It is old military cemetery with tidy white grave markers that is still managed by the Federal mortuary service at Fort Lewis. Some psychics' sense odd  feelings in the woods next to the cemetery and in the evening hours it is a great place to get photographs of orbs. Keep the camera stationary, perhaps use a tripod, and take a series of 20 or so pictures. One photographer who did this was rewarded with images of dozens of orbs that seemed to move around the graveyard as the images moved from one shot to another. These orbs were not visible during the shoot, but showed up on the pictures.

According to local legend a guard accidentally shot himself in the guard house (now the information/gift shop) when the fort was active. The soldier is reported to be still on guard duty long after his death. People have reported seeing "sparkles" in the guard house, but these sparkles do not appear on film. The "sparkles" are colorful and some are rather large, perhaps the size of a baseball. This anomaly seems to respond to voice introductions by an investigator which prompts a display. Many orbs such as the one pictured here are photographed at the guard building and an image of a blue apparition was taken there that can be viewed at www.hollowhill.com.

On Officers Row ghosts have been spotted in the original commander's house on the corner overlooking the water. The duplex buildings are numbered and the westernmost address of each building is noted with the letter W, easternmost with E for East. Researchers may want to start at the end of the street nearest the water at the Commanding Officers House. The photo of an apparition in that house was featured in an August 2005 Port Townsend Leader newspaper article. The building was made in the early 1900s'. The smell of burning coal or hot burning sulphur or burning rubber has been reported near the floor near a doorway. The Fort Worden maintenance workers cannot find the source.

Building 11W used to be officers quarters. A woman was staying overnight and in the middle of the night woke up to feel a presence in her bedroom. She felt a cold wave pass over her body from beneath the covers that were covering her.

Building 5W on Officers Row has had doors and windows open and close on their own accord. The current buildings that occupy the area on the side of the parade field across from Officers Row were originally barracks for the enlisted men.

During the 1950'-1970' the upper part of the fort was used as a State reform school. Building 201 held the detention cells for the particularly unruly residents and seems to be a popular spot for ghosts to hang out. The buildings are now used as dormitories.

An undisclosed 2 bedroom NCO quarters with two baths were being occupied by an elderly couple who retire to their queen sized bed. The wife was awakened when she felt something sit on the edge of the bed. Her husband was lying on the other side of the bed, sound asleep. Alexander's Castle dominates the parade ground and was built by before the Fort was commissioned. Ghostly happenings and sightings have been reported there.

Alexander's Castle dominates the Fort Worden hillside close to a firing battery position. This castle looking structure was built

before the Fort was established. John Alexander was the rector of the St Paul Episcopal Church in 1882. He built this home to serve as a residence for his intended bride who was still in Scotland. When he traveled to Scotland to pick her up, he found her married to another man. The castle, designed to catch rain water, is the oldest structure on Fort Worden and has been used as a residence, a tailor shop and an artillery observation post. Ghostly orbs have been photographed around the castle and sounds have been heard within the building when no one is inside.

Photographers can have a certain amount of success capturing orbs and ghosts with cameras on Fort Worden. Some hot spots to check out are the Guardhouse, the tree in front of the guardhouse (see orb photo on right) Dorm 201, 202 and 203, Alexander's Castle, the battery near castle and the school house. Images can be viewed at that web site. Photographs of housing units and the parade ground

show orbs and on at least one occasion the blue image of a man in front of a housing unit was observed. Further investigation is warranted for the guard house, parade ground and housing units. Check the ghostly images at www.aisling.net/artfest/04/ghosts.htm.

Prosser - Whitstran – A hill along the canal is called gravity hill because if a car is in neutral it will roll uphill and powder on the car may reveal fingerprints. Some people report seeing the face of a girl inches away from the persons face inside a truck. The face was an outline of eyes with long black hair over her face as if she had come out of a canal or water. At the time of the report the canal was dry. In another instance a student observed a woman with long black hair jump into the canal off of a little bridge that crosses the canal. Students at the hill turned off their ignitions of their cars and their cars began to move. When they looked back they reported seeing a young woman who was trying to push the car, as if she wanted them to leave. Rumor had it that in a barn near gravity hill some girls were raped and killed.

Purdy - -In the late seventies a child was hit by a car on the Purdy bridge. Occasionally people report seeing the image of a child darting across the bridge although his appearance is unpredictable.

Puyallup – At the Puyallup Fairgrounds the large Ferris wheel starts going and one of the seats start to rock and screaming is heard from time to time.

Queets- At the Native American Burial Ground several people visiting the burial ground have reported hearing strange noises resembling the beat of drums and Indian singing.

Renton - Maple Valley Highway is a very dangerous and dark road and there have been many accidents there. Witnesses report driving the road late at night and experiencing unexplained fog. Right after they pass through the fog they report seeing a crying teenage girl standing along side the road. She appears to be looking for a locket that was lost in the car accident that stole her life. Along Maple Valley Highway there is an old deserted haunted house that has lights go off and on by themselves even though there hasn't been electrical service in the house for years.

Legend has it that a janitor at Renton High School raped and murdered a girl and hung her body from the rafters in the old auditorium. She would make herself known only to small groups as she would play the piano, turn off the lights and sometimes manifest the balcony. She is said to haunt the 4th floor and the tower which is now off limits to students.

Downtown Renton McClendon's at 440 Rainier Ave S Renton. This was the old K-Mart, but before that it was Renton Hospital. People have reported unusual happenings there.

Sedro Wooley- The Cascade Job Corps was formerly the Northern State Hospital. This mental institution was used in the early 1900's and was the first institution to do a frontal lobotomy. There are supposedly over 1,000 unmarked graves in the back. Mischievous spirits have caused pans to fly off racks and lights to go off and on.

Seattle- Pike Place Market (1508 Pike Place) There are at least three separate ghosts who haunt the market. An old Native American woman, a young boy and an African American man have been reported at various levels and locations of this historic market... The market is haunted by the ghost of a Native American woman who has been seen in the market at night when all the tourists and shoppers have gone home. Reports of Princess Angelina in the Down Under area of the market prevail. She is sometimes referred to as the white lady and her eyes are a very bright blue. The market was built on a site that was sacred to the local Indians.

The Pike Place Market also harbors a ghost of a child at the Bead Emporium. When renovations were done to this business a few years ago, a basket of beads was discovered within the wall even though there was no access for this space, as the door had been painted shut many years before the store opened. Thread has been unraveled and beads are sometimes thrown at customers. Beads have fallen off their hooks and objects seem to find their way to new spots in this childlike, mischievous haunting. The ghostly child seems to enjoy playing the cash register from time to time, and a new puppet shop seems to have attracted the boy who seems to visit the marionettes in the evening.

Madam Nora presided over the Temple of Destiny in the early days of the market. This prophetess would practice crystal gazing, Indian psychic projection and Egyptian sand divining. Someone brought a crystal ball to the Pharaohs Treasure on the minus 2 levels and wanted to trade the crystal for something, not to take money. The trader mumbled something about a strange market woman who lived in the crystal ball. The ball sites among scarabs in this Egyptian shop and the owners report that sometimes they find that things have moved around in the night.

At Shakespeare's Books the same book was found on the floor at opening time by the owner's mother. The book would be dusted off and replaced on the shelves, only to find the book on the floor the next morning. The book was eventually destroyed. A few years later an author wrote a story while sitting at a desk in the same place the book had ended up on the floor. She did not know about the ghostly book at the bookstore, yet in the beginning of the book she describes the same ghost in the bookstore.

A very fat woman barber used to lull her clients to sleep and then rob them. She died when the floor gave way beneath her and she fell through. Some people in Pike Place Market have claimed that they have heard her ghost trying to lull people to sleep.

Frank Goodwin was a real estate developer and Market Director who built much of the early market. His upper level office is now the Goodwin library and there are reports that he frequents the site of his office.

There are fighting spirits in the meat locker of a Greek deli as well and janitors cleaning the lower levels of the market report hearing singing after hours.

Tours last about an hour and cost $10-12 Michael Yaeger may be contacted at Studio Solstone- 206-624-9102 or 206-682-7453. Or Sheila Lyon at 206-713-8506.

Kells Irish Pub is located in Post Alley at 1916 Post Alley is part of the Pike Place Market district. It used to be the embalming room for one of Seattle's oldest mortuaries.

Seattle - Belltown

Fire and Ice, 1921 First Avenue was built in 1903 as ER Butterworth's Mortuary. It is located on Second Avenue in Belltown between Stewart and Virginia. It is an active ghost haunt where investigators have reported over a dozen different spirits. Belltown's Butterworth Building houses odd apparitions. It is currently being renovated as the Starlite Lounge. At the corner of 1st and Virginia, near the Landes Building (Virginia Inn) tourists who look towards the sound will be rewarded with a beautiful view that is worth a picture or two.

The Cherry Street Coffee House is at 2721 1st Avenue at the corner of First and Clay. It is a12 story building with shops on the ground floor and apartment above.

Originally, the city morgue for Seattle, it had been turned into a first class restaurant called Avenue One and now is the home of the Cherry Street Coffee Lounge. This restaurant is on a prime corner and was an upscale steak house, then a Fine French Bistro, then a Thai

Restaurant. Diners may not realize that they are sitting in the former chapel of one of Seattle's early mortuaries. Perhaps that is one reason why so many businesses come and go on this corner. The corner of Broad and First has a spectacular view of the space needle

that seems to pop out of no where and should not be missed by tourists.

The Josephinum, 1902 Second Avenue near Stewart was an ornate hotel built in 1902.

This fourteen floor building is now owned by the Catholic Church and used to house elderly people. It is said to be filled with ghosts and residents talk about "the woman on the stairs".

The Moore Theater is located at 1932 Second Avenue at Virginia and Second Street. The Theater just looks as if it should be haunted, and it probably is. Employees who worked at the theater attempted to have a séance after hours until they were discovered by the owner, who fired them. The owner later reported hearing heavy breathing from an unseen visitor.

Rivoli Apartments, 2127 Second Avenue near Blanchard is the home of the Trundle Bed ghost. This specter is supposed to be the spirit of an Eskimo woman who was murdered there in the 1980s and hidden in one unit's trundle bed. Other ghosts include Christine, a former resident who used to clog her toilet to get attention and who social workers tried to get her to move to a permanent hospital. Christine has been send and felt by various tenants. Two residents who died of AIDS are said to inhabit the building standing guard over those who reside there. The Rivoli is a turn-of-the-century building, where the spirit of a young Eskimo girl who came to Seattle to start a new life has been felt and seen. She was stabbed to death by her mentally ill Cuban boyfriend and her body was hidden behind a Murphy bed. The door to her apartment was padlocked, and so she wasn't discovered for several weeks until her neighbor noticed a strange smell.

Sit-n-Spin at 2219 Fourth Avenue between Bell and Blanchard has the ghost a man who was involved in Seattle's politics in the 30's. A silhouette of a man in a Fedora hat was seen on the wall above the stage when the back room was opened. Psychics have felt things that coincide with the spirit on the wall. The ghost that haunts the club and Laundromat is said to be that of former Lt. Governor, Vic Meyers.

The Crocodile Café is located at the corner of 2nd Avenue and Blanchard at 2200 2nd Avenue in Belltown. Do past customer's still remain here?

Lava Lounge is found at 2226 Second Avenue near 2nd and Bell. This was an old sea farers bar that later became known as Hawaii West. Customers reports sounds of unearthly visitors from time to time.

The Rendezvous Lounge at 2320 Second Avenue is in Belltown near Battery Street and Second Avenue. It was built in 1922 and held a speakeasy and a movie house. Movies were shown at the Jewel Box Theater where the ghost is said to occupy the projection booth just above the door to the theater. Visitors have reported seeing an old card dealer lurking around the property on Friday and Saturday nights. Legend has it that the old card dealer is the spirit of Jimmy Durante, the only card player to ever be evicted from the club.

Seattle - Pioneer Square

Pioneer Square was Seattle's first neighborhood and laid the foundation for the rest of the city. It was in front of the Doc Maynard place that Chief Seattle addressed Governor Stevens who had been chosen as commissioner of Indian Affairs for the Washington Territory in 1854. Chief Seattle's words seem prophetic to ghost hunters as he explained that the commissioner should treat the Indians well. As Chief Seattle said:" And when the last red man shall have perished from the earth and his memory among white men shall have become a myth, these shores shall swarm with the invisible dead of my tribe, and when your children's children shall think themselves alone in the field, the store, the shop, upon the highway or in the silence of the woods they will not be alone."

Early Pioneer Square, it seems, was built on tidal flats that were regularly flooded with sea water, creating a quagmire in which horses and even children sank to their demise. In 1889 Seattle's Great Fire of 1889 leveled most of the city and the founders raised the city streets to provide drainage. These raised streets were eventually covered and enclosed and the lower chambers were eventually sealed off, forgotten and used only by vagrants, bootleggers and women of low repute. At census time the local prostitutes would identify themselves as seamstresses. So the city instituted a sewing machine tax!

In April 1854 a lynch mob hanged two Snohomish Indians on a stump at 1st and Main. The mob felt that the Indians had murdered a Pennsylvania man and buried his body on the shore of Lake Union. Sailors retrieved a block and tackle from their ship at Yeslers wharf and the mob broke into the cabin where the two accused Indians were being held, dragged them to the street corner and hanged the men. A third Indian of the party was held at a different location, tried, and found to be innocent.

Seattle's first hotel, the Felker House, was built on 1st Avenue and Main Street. It was run by Mary Ann Conkle who later added a brothel to the top floor. Mary Ann died in

1873 and the hotel burned to the ground in the Great Fire of 1889. Mary Ann is buried in Lake View Cemetery beneath a simple stone that attests to her personality in life. It reads: "Mother Damnable Conklin".

The Seattle Underground Tour starts at Doc Maynards 608 1st Avenue between Cherry and Yesler in Pioneer Square. Doc Maynard's is a restored 1890s pub that is reported to be haunted by a ghost that doesn't like music. During the tour the ghost of another man dressed in formal attire as well as a bank guard have been reported.

Tourists gather at a Doc Maynard's where they meet their guide. The guide explains that Pioneer Square has a history of plumbing catastrophes, scandals and misadventures. Participants are guided into parts of the city fourteen feet below the current streets. The tourists get to climb through old abandoned areas, explore history and learn of some of the more seedy parts of town and some of the ghostly activities that tend to happen there.

This year round tour takes about 90minutes, costs about $11 which must be paid in cash. The schedule varies, and is first come/first served. You can get information 206-682-4646 or check them out at www.undergroundtour.com.

Seattle - Capital Hill

The Capitol Hill Methodist Church holds a presence of Rev Daniel Bagley and his wife Susannah that haunts the parsonage of this church. One report states that a resident saw Susannah surrounded by a bluish light in a flowing gown. The spirit asked the resident "How do I get out?" The resident pointed to the door, but Susannah serenely floated out the upstairs window instead.

The Harvard Exit Theater is located at 807 East Roy in the Capital Hill Area. This movie theater used to be a meeting hall for the Women's' Century Club, a women's organization of the 1920's. People have reported seeing the ghost of a hanging woman in the hallway, as well as hearing footsteps and laughter. Sightings of several women in turn of the century clothes occur on the third floor and other sightings also occur in a first floor fireplace. A beautiful translucent woman wanders the lobby and stairwells, sometimes crying. Furniture is rearranged by ghostly spirits during the night, as if they were still having their meetings in the hall. Reports of a hanging woman in the hallway as well as footsteps and laughter have been reported. Local ghost hunters have investigated this theater and found anomalies such as the orb pictured here which seems to have a face in it. The face has been said to resemble that of the head of the Century Club, Ms. Landes.

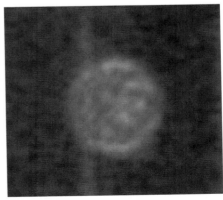

The Burnley School of Art was located at 905 E Pine Street at the corner of Broadway and Pine. There is a story that a young male student at Burnley committed suicide there, or fell to his death on the schools steep

rear stairway. Since that time his spirit has haunted the building by moving objects and pushing them off shelves. Some folks have claimed to see his ghost. Doors open by themselves, footsteps of invisible beings, phones dialed by unseen fingers and coffee percolating without human assistance in older style coffee makers have been reported. Furniture is mysteriously stacked or rearranged overnight in the empty and locked school.

When a medium attempted to contact the spirit in the 60's a loud crash was reported in the upstairs bathroom. Investigators found a broken window and a huge rock that was too heavy to have been thrown from the alley below. Investigators using "automatic writing" led them to the schools basement and a hole into which the rock fit perfectly. Further excavation revealed a small animal's skeleton, but no other reasons for such a disturbance. During a 1968 séance references were made regarding a left shoelace. At the conclusion of the séance it was revealed that the left shoelace of every male attendee of the séance had broken that day.

This site now houses a Dental Office and the English Institute of Seattle Central Community College. An interesting side note is that a statue of Jimmi Hendrix is located one block North on Broadway and is worth taking a look at. Jimmi is buried in the Greenwood Memorial Park in Renton.

The Sorrento Hotel is located at the corner of Madison and Terry Street at 900 Madison in Capital Hill. It is near the Emergency Room of the Virginia Mason hospital and cross the street from the hotel is the Puget Sound Blood Bank. In the Hunt Club Bar

165

(900 Madison) footsteps may be heard and glasses move in full view of the guests. An apparition of a woman has also been sighted on the 4th floor near room 408.

15th Avenue Video on 400 15th Avenue E (One block away from Funeral Alternatives which is at 526 15th Avenue) was an old fire house that still has the original "flip-open" fire truck doors in front. Four different employees have reported spooky

forms and swinging staff doors. One employee saw an apparition of a man in old garb striding across the main room

The Baltic Room is located at 1207 Pine Street in the Capital Hill district. It is located at the corner of Pine and Melrose. Male and female ghosts have been seen at this South Hill club.

Seattle - University District

University YMCA 5003 12th Ave was built in 1951 at the crossroads of 50th and 12th. After all members have left the building and the cleaning crew is cleaning the basement workout room footsteps and voices seem to come from the empty upstairs

area. A presence has also been felt in the furnace room.

College Inn Pub- 4006 University Way NE University District – Howard is a local ghost who appears as an old codger in a khaki trench coat to knock back a few beers. Reports of a piano playing without anyone sitting at the keyboard have been made and sightings of an Irish man have been reported in the back room.

The University of Washington Columns Amphitheater is so named due to the four columns of the original University of Washington building that was located closer to the downtown area. A young appearing male adult hangs around as a spirit that seems to dislike visitors. The entity is said to prey on couples sitting on a bench by shaking the shrubbery violently and growling. Some visitors feel uneasy entering the amphitheater at night with brooding feelings of foreboding coming over them.

The Neptune Theater 1303 Northeast 45th (at NE 45th and 13th Ave

NE) in the University District Corner of 45th and Brooklyn- unexplained cold spots and the smell of tobacco that is unseen have caused some people to name this haunting "The Smoking Ghost". Workers in the backstage area report the smell of

burning tobacco when no one is smoking in that area, and a ghostly image of a woman has been reported in the lobby.

Seattle - Georgetown

Central Baptist Church is at 1201 Ellis Street and the intersection of Ellis and Bailey. This Georgetown building was built in 1927 by the Masons and is the site of mysterious sounds, slamming doors. Sightings of a strange old man who haunts this Korean Baptist church have been reported. This was a former Masonic church which was supposedly used to  sacrifice animals and possibly even humans in the early days. Across the street from the stone marker that reveals the buildings age is a psychic shop called Spirit Quest with interesting wares and services. Travelers may want to stop by and speak with Janice and Lewis.

The Georgetown building that resembles a castle is located at 5501 Airport Way at the corner of Airport Way and Lucille. This  building once housed a brothel and a bar. It became an artist's co-op when these businesses left. The tattoo shop at the entrance once had a bar that ran along the left wall. A female ghost has been heard and seen on the property. At the Castle a crazy old lady has been seen choking herself with one hand and hitting witnesses with the other. Her eyes have been said to 'burn like coal'. The lady is believed to be a Spanish woman who killed her illegitimate babies and buried them under the porch. It may be Sarah, the spiritual survivor of a deadly loves triangle in the former Georgetown bordello.

Both Georgetown locations are located directly beneath the flight path of Boeing Field. Seattle's first airplane flight took place in Georgetown at the Meadows Race Track just south of Georgetown on the Duwamish River on March 11, 1910 under the skillful control of Charles Hamilton. Legend has it that a lumber magnate, William Boeing, observed the flight from the Duwamish river, where his yacht was being built. Apparently the founder of the Boeing Airplane Company was not around when Mr. Hamilton crashed his rickety Curtis Reims Racer aircraft into a pond two days later. Two years later in May of 1912 the same race track witnessed Seattle's first aviation death as J. Cliford Turpin was demonstrating his aero plane when it crashed into the grandstands, killing one person and injuring 21 others.

In February 1943 one of Boeings top secret XB-29 Super fortress bombers took off from Boeing field. This aircraft would eventually become the B-29 which would turn the tide in the Pacific and drop Atomic bombs on Japan in 1945. Twenty minutes after takeoff this secret aircraft's engine caught fire and Pilot Eddie Allen turned to land the aircraft at the field. A second fire erupted and two crewmen bailed out as the aircraft narrowly missed skyscrapers in downtown Seattle. Their chutes did not deploy in time and they perished. The giant bomber slammed into the Frye meat packing plant just short of Boeing Field, killing the nine remaining crewmen and as many as 30 workers in the plant.

In July 1949 a C-46 airliner from Air Transport Associates crashed in Georgetown killing two passengers and five people on the ground. Seven Georgetown homes were destroyed and

39 citizens were injured. The unscheduled flight carried 28 military passengers when the left engine lost power on take off. Circling around the field to return to the airport, the plane cut through two power lines and headed into the residences on Harney Street in Georgetown where five people in a wood frame rooming house at 961 Harney Street were killed. The cause of the accident was the use of the wrong type of fuel.

In August of 1951 another airplane tragedy struck as a Boeing B-50 bomber took of from the field, flying over Georgetown. While all engines were operating, the bomber seemed to lose power, turned toward the Ranier Brewery where it struck the top of the building and cart wheeled into the Lester Apartments (which has its own rich and salty history) on Beacon Hill, killing a total of 11 people.

Metropolitan Seattle

The Aurora Bridge is the large bridge that goes over Lake Union and carries drivers on Highway 99. Formally known as the George Washington Memorial Bridge it was dedicated in February of 1932 and spans Lake Union between the Fremont and Queen Anne  neighborhoods. The bridge is 167 feet above that water. The photo shown here is the last tall ship to make it out of Lake Union before the bridge closed the Lake to Tall Ships.

This bridge is also known as Suicide Bridge where people have killed themselves by hurling themselves off the great height. People have seen past suicides recreating their last dive on the bridge. It is said that a man jumped off the bridge with his dog to end both of their lives. People claim to still be able to see the chalk marks on the cement and early in the mornings, about 2-4 am, you may see the image of a man and a dog on the cement staring blankly.

In November of 1998 the worst bus accident in Seattle Metros 25 year history took place as the driver (Mark McLaughlin) of a southbound bus was shot twice by a passenger as the bus was crossing Aurora Bridge. 43 year old Silas Cool for unknown

reasons shot the driver with a 38 automatic, and then turned the pistol on himself. As the bus goes out of control, it drops 50 to land on the roof of an apartment building and tumbles to the ground near the Fremont Troll. (The Fremont Troll is a large sculpture underneath the north end of the bridge and worth a photo stop.) Killed in the crash were the driver, the shooter and one passenger, while 32 other passengers were injured.

Employees at the Claremont Hotel have reported sounds of a violent, riotous party from the 1920's and the Prohibition era complete with period jazz music and the sounds of breaking glass. Visitors have experienced a levitating paperweight, which crashed back to the glass-covered top of the desk. The staff has become painfully aware of the manifestations, and most have started to notice them. When staff members investigate the disturbances, which seem to come largely from the 9th floor, the noise abruptly stops, only to start up again later. A worker fell to her death from the hotel's upper floors in the 1960's, possibly adding to the ghostly air of the place. Complaints about the noise are common among hotel guests. A couple staying at the hotel reported seeing an apparition of a woman in their room.

Hamilton Middle School (1610 N.41st St) Hamilton Middle School seems to be very haunted. Many sightings take place when people are alone in the bathroom on the 2nd floor. Rumors of a student getting pregnant and dying at the school persist. Strange footsteps may be heard and doors open and close on their own at this school that may have its own version of night school.

171

The Green Lake area (5701 E Green Lake Way) is the scene of ghosts and apparitions that have been seen by numerous people. Some venture that it may be the ghost of some one who died in the lake. Gaines Point on the north end

of Green Lake was named in memory of Sylvia Gaines whose body was discovered on the north end of Green Lake on June 17, 1926. Sylvia was born in Massachusetts in 1904 and her parents split up five years later when Wallace Bob Gaines moved to Washington. By 1925 Sylvia had graduate from Smith College and came to visit Seattle to get to know her father. Within ten months she had been murdered.

The case was riveting to the community 80 years ago. Her father reported his daughter missing, and later identified her at the morgue. The prosecutor believed the fathers story that a fiend had raped and killed Sylvia. This theory began to unravel as investigators found that no neighbors or people walking by the lake had heard any commotion. This indicated that Sylvia

was not killed by some stranger, but rather by someone she had no reason to fear. But who had she been able to befriend in her short time in Seattle? Witnesses reported seeing Bob Gaines at the lake shore around 9pm that evening, near where the body was found. He had been seen bending down over something at the time. Other witnesses claimed to have seen Gaines drive around the lake several times at the time of the murder. Could the father have been the murderer?

After further investigation, the county Prosecutor, Ewing Colvin, began to lay out the case against the prime suspect - a World War I Veteran… Sylvia's father! A father, the brother of William Gaines who was the chair of the King County Board of Commissioners, was charged with the murder of his own daughter. Newspapers had a field day and wasted no time pointing out that Ewing was a good friend of the accused brother as the prosecutor investigated the death of the attractive 22 year old woman.

A jury of nine men and three women was chosen. In 1920 women had received the vote, but many states still did not allow them to sit on a jury until as late as 1940. The media attention was so intense that the judge ordered the jury to be sequestered in a Seattle hotel to hear the sordid details that lead to Sylvia's demise. She had been strangled and her head battered with a blunt instrument. Police found a bloody rock near the murder site. Testimony established that she had been murdered in one spot and then her body had been dragged several yards away and arranged in a way that would suggest a sexual assault.

The prosecutor discovered the motive for the murder. It appeared that Bob Gaines had an unnatural relationship with his new-found daughter for most of Sylvia's visit. They had not seen each other since she was five years old and she moved in with her father and his second wife.

They lived in the small one-bedroom house at 108 N 51st Street. At first Sylvia slept on the couch in the living room. The trio argued frequently as Mrs. Gaines became distraught over the

situation, even attempting suicide in 1925 when Silvia and her father threatened to leave the home and get their own apartment.

A neighbor believed that Sylvia and Gaines were sharing a bed and that Mrs. Gaines had been sleeping on the couch. A Seattle patrolman reported that he had discovered Gaines and his daughter late a night in Woodland Park, not half a mile from the house and half way between the house and Green Lake. The couple had been parked in Gaines car as teenaged lovers might have been. An employee of a downtown Seattle hotel testified that she had seen Gaines and his daughter in their nightclothes together in bed in November 1925. Witnesses described angry quarrels that erupted between Gaines and Sylvia in public. The prosecutor felt that Sylvia wanted to leave the house and stay with her uncle and that Bob Gaines had killed her to keep her from leaving him or revealing the incestuous affair.

Gaines testified that he had quarreled with Sylvia and she left the home at 108 N 51st street shortly after 8pm in an angry mood to walk around the lake. He swore that he drove around the nearby streets looking for her and then drove to the home of his friend and drinking companion, Louis Stern about 9:30pm. His alibi proved his undoing, as Louis Stern took the stand and reported that Gaines had told him "You know what I have always told you, that if anyone in my house told me when I should come and go and when I should drink and how much, why I would kill em… Well, that's what happened"

Colvin's closing argument stressed that Gaines had been sexually involved with his daughter for some months and that she was fed up and wanted to leave. On June 16 they quarreled and Sylvia left the house to get away from her father. Gaines found her walking near Green Lake and killed her in an alcoholic jealous rate. He then tore her clothes, dragged her body hearer the path and arranged the body in such a way as to suggest that she had been raped. He continued to drink heavily and confessed the murder to his drinking buddy, Louis Stern.

The jury took less than four hours to find Gaines guilty and sentence him to die. His unsuccessful appeal ended in his being hanged on August 31, 1928 in Walla Walla, Washington.

The community planted cottonwoods on the north end of Green Lake and called the area Gaines Point, to commemorate the death of the 22 year Sylvia Gaines. The trees grew for 70 years and provided roosting places for bald eagles and other birds. In 1999 the Park Department replaced the trees with poplars, thereby removing the last physical reminder of the tragedy, which may account for the reports of a female ghost who has been seen haunting Green Lake.

The Martha Washington Institute was a Women's' Institute located at 6612 57th Avenue South in Seattle. The story goes that sometime in the 40s-50s a janitor at this women's institution went crazy and murdered several patience and some staff before being subdued by police. It is said that he carried the bodies to a near by dock and threw several into the water. Psychics report bad spirits at the ruins of this institution, where girls were mistreated and babies were supposedly dropped into a well. People claim to see a faint shadow of a boy next to a tree. Some investigators claim that they explored the foundation, dock and small forest that remain. During their exploration one of the members was grabbed by the ankles by an invisible force that left scratches around the sock area. They claimed to hear footsteps and the crying of a woman or child. They report that the locals don't go near it and cursed them when they asked for directions.

SeaTac

The Radisson hotel is located at 17001 Pacific Highway (Hwy 99) at

the Southwest corner of Hwy 99 and 170th. Across 170th to the North is the Washington Memorial Park Cemetery. This hotel was built over part of the Washington Memorial Cemetery. The bodies were never removed, only the headstones. The ghosts of the people who were left under the hotel make an appearance in one certain wing of the hotel. Look for the wing closest to the present cemetery. Guests will often hear two people talking outside their doors, but when they go to investigate, they will see no one in the halls.

Examine the line pine tree at the West end of the Radisson parking lot, and then look at the pine trees across the street in the cemetery.

They are the same type and age. Visitors may want to check out the Raddisons restaurant, where they still serve spirits as indicated below.

Skykomish- Skykomish Hotel is the home of the "blue lady". During the railroad boom in the area the top floor was a speakeasy with a gambling parlor where ladies of the evening entertained their guests. One of the prostitutes' new boyfriend walked in on her as she was conducting business. The boyfriend had forgotten what her line of business was and killed her in a fit of rage. This old hotel has been unused for some time with a quilt shop on the lower floor and occasionally a restaurant will operate on the ground

floor. The upper floors are the rooms for guests and it is reported that room 19 is especially active, while some report that there may be more than one ghost here, and that "some of the old gals are still plying their trade".

Snohomish- At the Cabbage Patch Restaurant a nine-year-old girl is said to have fallen to her death down a flight of stairs inside the building. She still walks up and down the stairs, according to some reports.

The Oxford Saloon at 913 First Street used to be an old saloon complete with ladies of the evening. There are three main bars that are family friendly until 9pm and all serve good food. The worn wooden floors and antique bar make it a good place to soak up the atmosphere. A framed photograph of an old time policeman, in a Keystone Cops style of uniform, is by the stairs. Officer Henry was killed in a bar fight and is now said to inhabit the downstairs ladies room. Psychics have reported sensing other spirits of working girls and a "john" from the old days when a brothel occupied the third floor. A former house madam has been sensed hanging around, as has a former bar owner that has been known to "slap a few fannies" or make things fly off the countertop.

Nighttime is the preferred time to see ghostly activity at the Maltby Cemetery. This is a private cemetery and they do not take kindly to trespassers.
People have reported that when they walk down the headstone paths and read the headstones, when they get to the end and start back a certain headstone changes from a grave marker to a magnificent headstone. The change is not readily apparent. Whispers in the wind and trees have been reported and the specter of a woman searching for her child. There is supposed to be a ghost that guards the entrance to the den, and some claim that anyone entering the den will lose their mind or never be seen again.

The Snohomish public library was built in the early 1900's. The first librarian died of unknown causes and her gravesite is unmarked. People say they see her ghost walking around in the basement. Many workers hear her footsteps downstairs after hours and some claim to have seen her ghost.

Spanaway- Spanaway Jr. High School: Lights flicker and alarms go off. At the Spanaway Lake Park it is said that children who have drowned in the lake may be heard playing in the play ground above the park at nighttime when the park is closed. A fisherman reported seeing the pale corpse of a missing girl who drowned floating four feet under water on the south side of the lake in the early morning.

It has been reported that a teen-ager was murdered in Spanaway Park.

Spokane- Cameo Catering Event Facility: Mysterious noises are heard here and levitations of assorted objects are seen, primarily in the basement. Men are heard talking when the building is empty. The building was a Masonic hall for years. It is assumed that members who have since died object to "guests" in the building, as their rites were secret.

At Bowdish Middle School - people see a blurry dark figure. Figures have been seen in a women's bathroom by the cafeteria and a figure roams the halls between 12:00 noon and 5:00 pm.

At the Carlyle Care Center people have reported seeing shadowy figures and multiple electronic disturbances. One woman reported hearing a little girl's laughter.

The Centennial Middle School used to be Park Junior High School. Students have witnessed an old woman with no legs floating around in the library, and there are supposedly a man and a young woman hanging from the ceiling at the side entrance.

At the Double Tree Hotel every night since Halloween 1998, a mysterious noise occurs from the 15th floor. People have also seen mysterious shadows at this hotel.

Fairchild Air Force Base has a KC 135 type tanker aircraft is supposed to be haunted by two people who died on it in flight. Reports persist of strange groaning, loss of power for short period of time and objects dropping from their secured points. Fuel leaks come and go. The weapons storage a ghost called "The Goat Man" has been seen by on duty Security Forces. In the Geiger Corrections Center a scream was recorded on tape in an empty floor, although no one heard the scream in person, it was recorded as an EVP.

At Home, Heart, and Friends an older woman wearing a long gray dress from the 1900's has been seen walking up and down the staircase

Monaghan Hall at Gonzaga University is the music building for the University. The structure used to be the private residence for James Monaghan. There are many strange occurrences since then, including the organ being played when no one is there and various musical instruments playing by themselves. People hear the haunting music some of the time. The culprit is believed to be the ghost of

Mr. Monaghan himself. Strangely enough, the music heard by witnesses is the song that was played at Monaghan's funeral. Growling noises and other unseen forces also make themselves known to unsuspecting individuals. In the 1970s, Father Leedale performed an exorcism to clear the building. It was obviously done in vain, because the haunting still occurs.

The Northwest Christian Colbert Campus is reported to be haunted by the ghost of old Mr. Altmeyer telling them to leave. Many mysterious occurrences have happened here.

Patsey Clarks restaurant is an old mansion converted into an elite restaurant. The old wine cellar is haunted by three ghosts. Many employees have reported that for no reason a specter will pick up objects, usually wine bottles, and throw them across the room.

At the St. Xaviers church the face of a dead nun has been reported in one of the windows. She appears to be standing with her face over a candle and screaming.

Stanwood- People who have lived next to the Stanwood Museum say that late at night, when the museum is closed, you can see a candle be lit and the curtains open and shut. Sometimes even driving by, you can see a curtain pulled back as though someone is peering out. When people stop to look, the curtain goes back, although no one is in the museum at the time.

In the Pioneer Cemetery a black figure has been reported towards the back of the cemetery near a tree that overlooks a memorial like headstone The specter breaks a tree branch about six inches thick and chased the visitors. Families around there have had strange happenings and sightings such as seeing lanterns in the graveyard held by unknown persons. Others have experienced the lanterns in their own yards, displaying a kind of light show. When people investigate the lights remain in place for a moment then start coming towards the investigators before they disappear.

Steilacoom- At the ER Rogers Restaurant many employees have reported abnormal occurrences within the building. There is a lot of history behind this mansion. One of the owner's wives killed herself in the mansion and still haunts it, but it has been reported that multiple ghost or entities reside there. At one time it was a bed-and-breakfast during the depression.

Tacoma - University of Puget Sound holds a dubious honor. It is widely believed that Ted Bundy killed his first victim and dumped her in the foundation of a building being built at the University of Puget Sound. Although her body was never found, people have reported seeing a girl - believed to be her - walking the halls of the building and making strange noises.

The deceased builder of the Thornewood Castle, Chester Thorne, has made several appearances over the years. After the lights were turned off and no one else was present, light bulbs will be unscrewed in his room. Some guests have seen Chester's wife, Anna, sitting in the window seat of her room overlooking the garden. Some have claimed to see her reflection in her original mirror in the room she occupied, which is now the Bridal Suite. The Thornes son in law shot himself in the gun closet. His ghost has been seen from time to time. Another ghost is of the grandchild of a former owner who drowned in the lake. Occasionally guests will rush down from our Grandview Suite concerned because there's a small child alone by the lake only to find no child there. A Stephen King miniseries titled "Rose Red" was filmed in Thornewood Castle and aired in February 2002.

Near the old Western State Sanitarium when the moon is full and on some rainy foggy nights it has been reported that people can hear moans and footsteps in the late night to early morning hours. This is believed to be patients that were once institutionalized there. The place is in ruins now, but there remains an underground boiler room where most the sounds are heard. The fence around the facility shakes for no reason when no one is around. There have been reports of cold spots, sounds of people and the cold sense of a presence. Reports include an image of blood on the wall reading JOE... a hand print and long dried blood that almost seemed to be dripping.

On 5 mile Drive in Point Defiance Park a little girl was riding her bicycle in the lat 1980's. She was murdered and her killer was never caught. Late at night the sound of a bicycle can be heard. One report states that a woman was driving on the road after the park was closed. As she rounded the turn near Narrows Viewpoint she saw what she thought was a young girl with a bicycle standing by the side of the road. When the woman stopped the car her boyfriend got out of the car to ask the little girl if she was okay. The boyfriend was frightened by the girl since she had no eyes and raced back into the car screaming at his girlfriend to drive away. As the car sped away the woman looked in the rearview mirror to see that little girl vanish.

Gog-li-hi-ti Wetlands - Just to the South of the Wetlands Park was one of the places where the Puyallup Indian tribe buried their dead, along the banks of the Puyallup River. Many people fishing there have seen a canoe paddled by a Native American pull up to the bank and then disappear. There have been reports of singing and voices near the river. The Army Corps of Engineers now fences off the area. Late at night workers and fisherman report an old man with a yellow dog walking the banks of the North Levee Road. People have reported seeing the man with an angry expression on his face. Sometimes a dog can be heard wailing from the site.

Hollywood on the Flats - immediately adjacent to the Wetlands, also known as "Hooverville". The last transient was evicted in 1952. The old transient, wearing a tan shirt and pants held the Pierce County Sheriff Deputies and Tacoma Police at bay with a shotgun, refusing to leave his "home". The standoff ended with a single gunshot when the man took his life rather than be evicted. His old yellow mixed breed Lab dog was heard wailing.

Old City Hall - Security guards there have reported elevators moving on their own accord, lights being turned off and on, and doors that were locked being checked and found unlocked.

Lakewood - There is a lake in the woods that is located behind Pierce College on the way to the old Western state sanitarium. At night and early morning hours you feel a presence, see hazy apparitions and hear voices around the lake. They may belong to a woman that drowned there many years ago.

Point Defiance Park - The Pagoda used to be the trolley terminus at Point Defiance in the early part of the 20th century. The building was remodeled and is now rented out for weddings/parties. Visitors, workers and the Police have reported hearing footsteps made with hard soled shoes walking around the building after dark. The footsteps seem to be walking down the stairs on the east side of the building, then abruptly stop. Sighing can be heard at other times and there are cold spots in the storage area below the building. A tale has been told about a young newlywed couple during the 1920's. The husband and wife would catch the trolley to Point Defiance and the husband would see his wife off for the day to visit her parents on Vashon Island. Small groups of boats would shuttle people to the island for a fee. The husband would return in the evening to meet his wife. As the small launch she was riding in approached the Boathouse area, it took on water. Many people were thrown overboard in the confusion and the husband observed with his pocket spyglass his wife flailing in the water in her heavy period clothes as she went under. Overcome with grief, he walked down the stairs to the marbled restroom, pulled out a small pocket pistol and shot himself in the head. It is said it is his ghost that haunts the Pagoda.

Puget Sound Mental Hospital is a large facility for the mentally disturbed (and a drug and alcohol rehabilitation center). Parts of this 8-story complex are no longer in use. Half of the facility lies in darkness and is used for storage or is closed off because it is "unsafe". All of the buildings of this facility are highly haunted. Most of the staff there are willing to tell tales of the many ghostly personalities that reside there. The most famous is that of an old woman and her walker that can be seen and heard going up and down the hallways of the 4th floor. This place is a working facility and visitors need permission to tour the campus.

University of Puget Sound - The Inside Theatre (the name may have changed in the past few years) is haunted by an unseen, but essentially benign presence. The ghost does not appear physically, but manifests itself by shifting scenery, turning on and off lights, slamming doors, rattling paint cans, etc. There is one case in which a student was leaning over the catwalk to change a light and lost her balance. She felt an unseen force jerk her backwards onto the catwalk, ostensibly preventing her from falling.

Thorp – Visitors to the Thorp cemetery have reported seeing the ghost of an Indian woman by the name of Suzy riding a white horse and crying among the tombstones on moonlit nights. She was lynched by unknown persons around 1890.

Toppenish – The Public Library / museum is haunted by a weird woman and man on the top floor that can be seen looking out the window.

Vancouver - Fort Vancouver was a trading post of the Hudson's Bay Company, the first settlement in the Pacific Northwest. At Fort Vancouver, the ghost of Dr. John McGloughlin still haunts his old house; they say you can hear his heavy foot steps walk up and down the halls. Some say there are people in the look out tower that can be seen from the ground.

The old army barracks are still occupied and are a stone's throw from the old Fort Vancouver. It is believed that the barracks were constructed over several old colonial graves and there have been stories of ghosts haunting the auditorium, the officer's housing, etc.

The Grant House is a part of Officer's Row, a strip of colonial style houses that was used for housing officers of the Vancouver Barracks since the mid 1800's. The Grant House was the first built and was once home to President Ulysses S. Grant during his tenure before his presidency. A former officer named Sully haunts the house. The ghost is even mentioned in the pamphlet at the front door. (The house is now a folk art museum and restaurant).

Officer's Row - There is a house two lots to the left of The Grant House on Officer's Row where visitors report that on Saturday through Tuesday the grass in front of the house is dead and brown. Inside the house there is a substance that looks like blood dripping from the walls. The local newspaper reported that a tenant's wife had spent hours scrubbing the walls and the blood continues to appear.

The third floor of the old Veterans Hospital used to house mentally disturbed patients. It is said that visitors can still hear their hysterical screams, and any paper that enters the room floats to the ceiling and sticks there.

Late at night in the gym of the former Fort Vancouver High School people report the sound of a ladder falling and a loud crash along with a man falling from what looks like thin air. Upon impact with the ground the people report hearing a loud crack... One teacher reported that when this happened the teacher saw bones poking out of the specter's neck just before he disappeared. According to rumor a maintenance man was putting up a basketball hoop n the 1930's when his ladder broke and he fell to his death.

Waitsburg - The Haunted Tunnel is said to be haunted by a ghost that walks the tunnel with its severed head and the machinery that killed him following behind.

Waterville There is an old school house that was built in 1864 a couple miles out of town where people report seeing candle light emanating from the shattered and boarded up windows. Neighbors report hearing children playing and the squeaking of a swing set that has long since been removed from the site. Flashlights and candles go out when people enter the main schoolroom.

Wenatchee- Cherub Bed & Breakfast Inn has an interesting history. A husband came back from vacation to find his wife cheating on him. The husband killed the other man on the stairs and it is reported that you can hear someone walking up and down the stairs when no one is there. There are also bloodstains on the stairs that disappear for a few moments when washed and then reappear.

Whidbey Island – At Fort Casey there are strange drawings on the walls and visitors report hearing something scratching on the walls. Figures and a woman screaming have also been reported.

White Swan – At the Old Fort Simco State Park witnesses have reported seeing a woman looking out of one of the back windows of the commanders' house. It is thought that she may be the wife of the commander who died of fever in the 1800s. The fort may be the source of the Toppenish ghost lights seen in the area in 1973.

Whitman – Visitors to the LaCrosse School may see a shadow of a person walking down the hallways hitting the lockers.

Woodinville- The Chateau Ste Michelle Winery Manor House is located on 150 beautiful acres that were previously owned by Seattle lumber and dairy baron, Fredrick Stimson. According to legend Mr. Stimson managed to get one of the servant girls pregnant. When Mrs. Stimson found out, the servant girl "fell" to her death down a back stairwell which leads to the kitchen. Shadows have been seen and cold spots have been felt. Noises have been heard and the spirit opens the upstairs restroom window, closes the door and lights go off and on. Late night cleaning staff has reported hearing footsteps when no one is there. Security systems malfunction.

Yakima – People have reported more than 100 times in Cherry Park children running around in circles screaming at the top of there lungs. This goes on for a good half an hour, while a strong scent of sulfur remains in the air.

Visitors to the 4th floor of St. Paul's School report hearing a little scream or seeing a little shadow of a lady who taught at St. Pauls 20 years ago. It is rumored that she jumped out of a window or died in an elevator. In the girls bathroom the sound of flushing and water turning on may be heard, even though no one is there. Near the morgue and around the elevator at Yakima Memorial Hospital people experience cold drafts and sees the elevator doors open and close. Out of the corner of the eye people report seeing someone walking, running or sitting down, but these people disappear when the person looks directly at the shadow.

Yakima canyon (about two miles north of the roza recreation area, on the left) is supposed to be haunted recently by a young Hispanic male who was murdered there and an elderly man with gray hair and beard that committed suicide in the same area.

Contacts

Like peeling an onion, ghost hunting leads to layer after layer of interesting material. The internet is a valuable resource and most ghost hunting organizations have photos and links to other sites to further research. Some of the basic sites are listed here.

Popular Web Sites:

WWW.AGHOST.US — Amateur Ghost Hunters of Seattle/Tacoma in Washington

WWW.GHOSTWEB.COM — International Ghost Hunters Society

WWW. GHRS.ORG — Organization of Ghosts and Hauntings Research Society

WWW.AAEVP.COM — American Association Electronic Voice Phenomena

WWW.GHOSTPIX.COM — Examples of EVP and photography

WWW.GHOST-VOICES.COM — A large collection of EVP

WWW.EVPVOICES.COM — A large collection of EVP

WWW.GHOSTVILLAGE.COM — Ghost research, evidence and discussion

WWW.AMERICANGHOSTS.COM — A compendium of ghostly locations

WWW.ZEROTIME.COM — Paranormal, ghosts and related information

WWW.RIPTX.DNS2GO.COM — Researchers and Investigators of the Paranormal lots of photos

WWW.THESHADOWLANDS.NET — Lists of haunted places

WWW.HAUNTSTER.NET — Anomalies with Attitude

WWW.MAGICKMIND.NET — Paranormal Talk Radio

WWW.GHOSTSANDCRITTERS.COM — Large collection of haunted locations

WWW.MARKETGHOST.COM — Seattle Pike Market Ghost Tours- usually 6pm

WWW.PRIVATEEYETOURS.COM — Seattle Ghost Tours by Jake in a motorized van

WWW.GHOSTMAG.COM — Ghost magazine site

WWW.HOLLOWHILL.COM — Images and information on Ft Worden

Websites about Infrasound:

http://www.meta-religion.com/Paranormale/Ghost/very_low_frequency.htm

http://www.borderlands.com/newstuff/research/infra.htm

http://www.csmonitor.com/2003/0918/p14s02-stss.html

http://geology.about.com/library/weekly/aa121497.htm

http://www.guardian.co.uk/Archive/Article/0,4273,4038891,00.html (A ghost story)

Websites by State

State	Name	URL
Alabama	Mystical Blaze	www.mysticalblaze.com
Alaska	Paranormal Photos.com	http://paranormalphotos.tripod.com
Arizona	Arizona Paranormal Invest.	www.arizonaparanormalinvestigations.com
Arkansas	The Spirit Seekers	www.thespiritseekers.org
California	Ghost Trackers	www.ghost-trackers.org
Colorado	All About Ghosts	www.allaboutghosts.com
Connecticut	Ghosthound	www.ghosthound.com/
Delaware	Paranormal Invest.	http://pages.zdnet.com/dprs/ghosts/
Florida	GHG Ghost Hunters	www.ghgghosthunters.com
Georgia	Ghost Force	www.ghostforce.com
Hawaii	Kwaiden	www.geocities.com/Area51/Hollow/6166
Idaho	Idaho Spirit Seekers	www.geocities.com/idahospiritseekers/index.html
Illinois	Ghost Research Society	www.ghostresearch.org
Indiana	Shadowchasers of NWI	www.nwishadowchasers.homestead.com
Kansas	Seekers of the unknown	http://seekersoftheunknown.homestead.com
Kentucky	Southern Paranormal Res.	www.southernghostresearch.org
Louisiana	The haunted traveler	www.hauntedtraveler.com
Maryland	Ghost & Spirit Assoc.	www.marylandghosts.com
Mass.	Cape and Island Assoc	www.caiprs.com
Michigan	Mid Mich. GHS	www.mmghs.com
Missouri	Missouri GHS	www.ghosthaunting.com
Nebraska	Grasping Shadows	www.geocities.com/graspingshadows
Nevada	NV Ghosts & Hauntings	www.ghrs.org/nevada/
New Jersey	South Jersey Ghost Res.	http//southjerseyghostresearch.org
New York	NY Ghost Chapter	www.newyorkghostchapter.com.
NC	L.E.M.U.R.	www.phantoms.cc
Ohio	Ohio Paranormal	www.angelfire.com/oh3/opin
Oklahoma	OK Ghost Patrol	http://okghostpatrol.net
Oregon	Pacific Paranormal	www.nwpprs.com
Pennsylvania	Cathes Ghost Encounters	http://hauntedfieldsofglory.com
Rhode Island	T.A.P.S.	http://the-atlantic-paranormal-society.com
South Carolina	Coastal Spirit Chasers	www.coastalspiritchasers.net
Tennessee	Ghosts of Tennessee	www.tnghost.org
Texas	Ghastly Ghost Hunter	www.ghastlyghosthunter.com
Utah	Utah Ghost Organization	www.utahghost.org
Virginia	Spheres of Influence	www.carfaxabbey.net/spheres
Washington	SeattleTacoma Ghost Hunt	www.aghost.us
	WA State PIR	www.wspir.com
West Virginia	WV Society of Ghost Hunt	www.wvsocietyofghosthunters.com
Wisconsin	SW Paranormal Research	www.paranormalresearchgroup.homestead.com

References

Ghost Stories of Washington
Lone Pine Publishing,

Barbara Smith 2000
Renton, Washington

How to Hunt Ghosts, A Practical Guide,
Simon and Shuster,

Joshua P. Warren 2003
New York, NY

Contact The Other Side

Konstantino

How to be a Ghost Hunter
Llewellyn Publications,
55164-0383

Richard Southall, 2003
St. Paul, Minnesota

Stories in Stone

Douglas Keister

Ghost Hunting, How to Investigate
The Paranormal
Ronin Publishing

Loyd Auerbach

Berkely, California

The UFO Investigators Handbook
Running Press, Philadelphia

Craig Glenday 1999

Forms

Any organization must maintain records of their activities in order to be considered legitimate. This record keeping is the drudgery of ghost hunting. While it is exciting to participate in the actual hunt, when investigators pack up and leave the haunted area the real work begins. The devil is in the details, they say. Pre-printed forms help to make this task a little easier.

The following pages include sample forms that can be used to simplify the ghost hunters' efforts when conducting an expedition, walk-through or an investigation.

Forms should be filled in as soon as possible after the event, and not later than two weeks after the event. Reports should be submitted to the team leader for consolidation and verification before being submitted to the organization and archived.

Proposal for Permission to Conduct a Field Investigation For ANY Cemetery or Place

Name
Organization
Address

To Whom It May Concern:

I represent AGHOST (Amateur Ghost Hunters of Seattle Tacoma), a group of researchers in the field of paranormal studies. As part of our ongoing education, we are researching historical sites, including cemeteries, churches, parklands, etc.

We seek permission to have access for 1 (ONE) evening, (date), after regular gate hours, for __ hours, from _ pm until __ pm, in order to conduct a field investigation using the following tools:
1. Photography (digital, standard and infrared)
2. Tape recorders
3. Flashlight, compass, spare film, batteries and tapes and other equipment as required.

Our research is dependent on clear weather, and will have to be postponed if fog, rain, high winds, snow or other inclement weather occurs on the set date and time. We will notify you of any cancellation. If there is a need to reschedule, your permission will again be sought.

We understand, and fully respect that we will be on private property at all times, and all due consideration will be given so that no damage come to any burial sites, mementos, or any part of your property. We each have the utmost respect for all those who have a loved one buried here, and solemnly promise there will be no intoxicant consumption, horseplay, or any other disagreeable conduct, just the research as mentioned above will be done, for the duration permitted, and on the agreed site(s).

We agree that we undertake this research at our own risk, and understand that your organization is not responsible for any injury or damage to the students or their instruments, while on your property. If you require any other conditions to be met, please provide them and we will incorporate into our proposal.

Yours truly,

_____

Your name
96 Main Street, City, State
Home: (555) 555-8772   Work: (216) 555-1224

Phone: _____**Email:** _____
Website: www.aghost.us

RESEARCH RELEASE FORM

I, _____, have the authority to allow access to AGHOST members and affiliated persons to _____ located at _____ for the purpose of conducting an investigation into possible paranormal occurrences or conducting field research at this location. The investigation process has been explained to me and I give AGHOST permission to conduct an investigation at this location. AGHOST releases the owner of the location from any liability for injuries and/or damages incurred during the investigation. AGHOST assumes responsibility for any damages to the property during the investigation.

Signed_____

Date _____

Print Name _____

Witness_____

Date _____

Print Name _____

RELEASE OF INFORMATION AND EVIDENCE

AGHOST respects your right to privacy. All of your personal information will be kept confidential. AGHOST is requesting to use some, or all, of the information and evidence collected during the investigation for possible inclusion in our website, newsletter and other future media considerations.

Please check the level of confidentiality you would like to request:

_____ AGHOST may not release any part of the investigation to the public.

_____ AGHOST may release information provided that the identity of witnesses and clients are changed and the exact address of the location are excluded.

_____ AGHOST may release any/all of the information and evidence collected during the investigation.

_____ Other

_____
_____
_____

Signed_____
Date _____
Print Name _____

Witness_____
Date _____
Print Name _____

AGHOST MEMBERSHIP AGREEMENT

I, _____, am requesting to join AGHOST, Amateur Ghost Hunters of Seattle Tacoma, (herein after referred to as Organization). I fully understand and accept all of the following terms and conditions of membership and agree as follows:

1. I will not hold the Organization or the Organization members, guests or private property owners liable for any physical or mental injury or accident to myself while I am on or participating in any walk-through, investigation, expedition, meeting or Organization activity.

2. I am not aware of any physical or mental impairment that would prevent my participation in Organization activities. I assume full responsibility for my own welfare and safety while participating in same.

3. I agree to respect confidentiality relative to other Organization members, private residences, property owners, etc., of any locations visited or discussed by the Organization. I will not give out information, including names, locations or details of walk-through or investigations to anyone outside of the Organization without express permission of the Executive Officers.

4. I will show respect for any site visited during an investigation or expedition, and understand that any destruction of property on a site will be grounds for loss of membership. I also understand I will be liable for any and all damages that I caused.

5. All walk-through, investigations and expeditions must be performed in a courteous and professional manner.

6. I will wear a valid official AGHOST membership badge to all walk-through, investigations, expeditions and formal Organization events.

7. I understand and agree that during my participation in any official Organization walk-through, investigations, expeditions, meetings or official Organization activities my likeness and/or voice may be captured in photos and/or videos and such photos and videos may be used for various purposes and I waive my right to compensation from the Organization.

8. I understand that any photographs taken by me may be used for my personal use and that by participating in the organization function I have given AGHOST the authority to use those images or recordings in any way they seem fit to include but not limited to publication in books, newsletters, web site or in electronic format.

9. I understand and agree that if I participate in a non-official event with other AGHOST members that I will not hold the Organization responsible for compensation for any use of my likeness and/or voice in photos and/or videos.

10. I accept that the onsite Team Leader is to make all decisions concerning the walk-through, investigations and expeditions. Failure to follow such directions will be grounds for termination of membership.

11. In the event that I conduct any investigations or expeditions on my own, I agree to assume full responsibility for my actions and will not involve the Organization in any manner.

12. I understand that seeking the truth is vital to the purpose of the Organization, and in line with this, I will not falsify ANY evidence, including photos, videos, information, etc.

13. Any contact with the media, i.e., interviews, giving information, pictures, etc., is strictly prohibited unless permission is obtained from the Executive Officers.

14. I further agree that any questions from the media, police or others that may arise on site during an actual investigation or expedition will be directed to the onsite Team Leader.

15. I will not bring any non-members to an investigation or expedition without the approval of the Organization President/Executive Officers.

16. I accept full responsibility for the actions of any non-members that I may bring to an investigation, expedition or meeting.

17. I agree to respect the dignity and rights of other Organization members, officers and Executive Officers even if I am not in agreement with their ideas or opinions, and will conduct myself at all times in a mature and adult manner. Obscene, foul or abusive language in any Organization activity is unacceptable.

18. I agree that there is to be no use of alcohol, drugs or illegal substances at any walk-through, investigation, expedition, meeting or formal Organization event.

19. I will not bring firearms or weapons to any walk-through, investigation, expedition, meeting or formal Organization event.

20. If I terminate my membership prior to payment renewal date, I understand that I will not receive a refund of any portion of dues previously paid.

21. If I reapply for membership in the Organization, I acknowledge that I will apply as a new member, will follow all rules for new membership and be responsible for payment of new membership fees.

I have read, understand and agree to abide by all of the By-Laws, policies, protocols and rules as a condition of membership in the Organization. I understand that failure to follow any of the By-Laws, protocols, policies or rules may be grounds for termination of my membership. The Organization reserves the right to terminate my membership at any time.

Print Name: _____

Signed_____ Date: _____

....

For AGHOST Use Only

Date of New Member Orientation: _____

Date Dues Paid: _____

Date Membership Activated: _____

Date Membership Badge Provided _____

NOTES:

_____

_____

_____

AMATEUR GHOST HUNTERS OF SEATTLE, TACOMA

197

AMATEUR GHOST HUNTERS OF SEATTLE, TACOMA

AGHOST MEMBERSHIP INFORMATION SHEET

Name:

(NAME WILL BE LISTED IN CONFIDENTIAL MEMBERS AREA OF THE AGHOST WEBSITE)

Address:

City: _____ **State** _____ **Zip:** _____

(ALL ADDRESSES WILL BE KEPT CONFIDENTIAL)

Home Phone/Cell Phone: _____ / _____

Work Phone: _____
(If you can be contacted at work)

Emergency Contact Name / Telephone Number:
_____ / _____

E-mail Address (es):

(EMAIL ADDRESSES WILL BE LISTED IN CONFIDENTIAL MEMBERS AREA OF THE AGHOST WEBSITE)

I give my permission to provide to other members and/or post in the members' only (confidential) area of Yahoo Groups and/or the AGHOST website my:

Cell phone number ___Yes ___No
Home phone number ___Yes ___No
Signed: _____ Date: _____

What interests you most about paranormal investigations?

_____
_____
_____
_____

Have you had any personal paranormal experiences? ___Yes ___No ___ Maybe

If so, please briefly describe:

_____
_____
_____
_____
_____
_____

Do you consider yourself to have some psychic ability? ___Yes ___No ___ Maybe
If so, please briefly describe:

_____
_____
_____
_____

If you have any abilities or knowledge that you think might benefit the group please list them below:

_____
_____

How did you find out about AGHOST?

_____
_____
_____

What influenced you to become a member?

_____
_____
_____

What are your expectations from your participation with the group?

_____

_____

Please list any other ghost hunting clubs and affiliations you are also a part of:

_____

_____

* NOTE

- Full name <u>will</u> be listed in the members' only [confidential] areas of Yahoo groups and/or the AGHOST website.
- First name and last initial will be used in any public areas of the website and all other instances unless permission to use the full name is given by the member.
- All addresses <u>will</u> be kept confidential and will be given out only with permission of the member.
- No telephone numbers will be provided to anyone outside of the Organization without the permission of the member.

Report Forms

Walkthrough Report

Investigation

Investigation type:
Basic ☐
Intermediate ☐
Advanced ☐

A.G.H.O.S.T.
AMATEUR GHOST HUNTERS OF SEATTLE, TACOMA

Date: (mm/dd/yy)
/ /
Start Time :
End Time :

Investigator:

Weather:
Moon Phase:
Solar X-Rays:
Geomagnetic:
AVG Temp:

Purpose:

Address:

Location Type:

Investigation Category:
Age of Property:
Owner History:

Investigators Present

Present Inhabitants (name and age)

Current Activity Report: _____

_____

Property History: _____

_____

_____

Traumatic History: _____

_____

Alleged Reason for Activity: _____

_____

_____

Tests run at this location: _____

_____

Results:

_____

_____

Observer Report

Investigation

Investigator:

A.G.H.O.S.T.

AMATEUR GHOST HUNTERS OF SEATTLE, TACOMA

Date: (mm/dd/yy)

/ /

Start Time :
End Time :

Outside Impression: _____
_____
_____
_____

Walk-in Impression: _____
_____

Room: _____
_____

Room: _____
_____

Room: _____
_____

Room: _____
_____

Room: _____
_____

Closing feelings: _____

Phenomenon Report

Investigation

Investigation type:
Basic ☐
Intermediate ☐
Advanced ☐

Investigator:

A.G.H.O.S.T.

AMATEUR GHOST HUNTERS OF SEATTLE. TACOMA

Date: (mm/dd/yy)
          /   /
Start Time   :
End Time   :

Type of Phenomenon

Visual ☐   Physical ☐   Heard ☐   Smelled ☐

What was going on just before the phenomena? _____

_____

_____

_____

Describe Phenomenon? _____

_____

_____

Your feelings at the time?_____

_____

Readings at the time? _____

_____

Witnessed by: _____

Identify video, photos and audio taken at the very same moment _____

_____

_____

Comments or closing thoughts: _____

_____

203

Tech Report

Investigation type:
Basic ☐
Intermediate ☐
Advanced ☐

Investigator:

Equipment Used:

A.G.H.O.S.T.
AMATEUR GHOST HUNTERS OF SEATTLE, TACOMA

Investigation

Date: (mm/dd/yy)
/ /
Start Time :
End Time :

Outside Impression:
_____
_____
_____

Walk-in Impression:
_____
_____
_____

Room: _____
_____

Room: _____
_____

Room: _____
_____

Room: _____
_____

Room: _____
_____

Structural Notes (attach floor plan): _____
_____

Closing feelings: _____
_____

Camera Log

Investigation

Investigator:

___

A.G.H.O.S.T.

AMATEUR GHOST HUNTERS OF SEATTLE, TACOMA

Date of tape:
(mm/dd/yy)

/ /

Start Time : AM☐ /PM☐
End Time : AM☐ /PM☐

Type of camera used _____
Film /ASA__ (remember to use 400 or higher speed)
Was strap removed or kept around your wrist for investigation?   YES☐ / NO☐
Was the lens cleaned before you started the investigation?   YES☐ / NO☐
Are you using a fresh roll of film?   YES☐ /NO ☐ (if not what's the starting #____)

Picture #_____ Time : AM☐ /PM☐
Description:
_____

Picture #_____ Time : AM☐ /PM☐
Description:
_____

Picture #_____ Time : AM☐ /PM☐
Description:
_____

Picture #_____ Time : AM☐ /PM☐
Description:
_____

Picture #_____ Time : AM☐ /PM☐
Description:
_____

Picture #_____ Time : AM☐ /PM☐
Description:
_____

Picture #_____ Time : AM☐ /PM☐
Description:
_____

205

E.V.P. Report

Investigation #

Investigator:

A.G.H.O.S.T.
AMATEUR GHOST HUNTERS OF SEATTLE, TACOMA

Date of Tape:
(mm/dd/yy)

/ /

Start Time :
End Time :

: : **Tape Time Code**

_____

_____
_____
_____

: : **Tape Time Code**

_____

_____
_____
_____

: : **Tape Time Code**

_____

_____
_____
_____

: : **Tape Time Code**

_____

_____
_____
_____

: : **Tape Time Code**

_____

_____
_____
_____

: : **Tape Time Code**

_____

_____
_____
_____

Suggestions or comments

Video Report   Investigation #_____

Investigator:

A.G.H.O.S.T.
AMATEUR GHOST HUNTERS OF SEATTLE, TACOMA

_____

Date of tape:
(mm/dd/yy)
__/ __/ __
Start Time __:__
End Time __:__

:   :   **Video Time Code   Type of Phenomena: Audio ☐ Visual ☐**

_____

:   :   **Video Time Code   Type of Phenomena: Audio ☐ Visual ☐**

_____

:   :   **Video Time Code   Type of Phenomena: Audio ☐ Visual ☐**

_____

:   :   **Video Time Code   Type of Phenomena: Audio ☐ Visual ☐**

_____

:   :   **Video Time Code   Type of Phenomena: Audio ☐ Visual ☐**

_____

:   :   **Video Time Code   Type of Phenomena: Audio ☐ Visual ☐**

_____

:   :   **Video Time Code   Type of Phenomena: Audio ☐ Visual ☐**

_____

:   :   **Video Time Code   Type of Phenomena: Audio ☐ Visual ☐**

_____

Suggestions or comments _____

Psychic Report

Investigation

Investigator:

AMATEUR GHOST HUNTERS OF SEATTLE, TACOMA

Date: (mm/dd/y)

/ /

Start Time :
End Time :

Outside Impression: _____

_____

_____

_____

Walk-in Impression: _____

Room: _____

Room: _____

Room: _____

Room: _____

Room: _____

Room: _____

Closing feelings: _____

Sample Press Release

(Should be one page and of interest to the media)

Working with the media can be a mixed blessing. Ghost hunting organizations can benefit from positive images, but a poorly written or detrimental article in the newspaper or television can crush an organizations morale and credibility.

As the media recognizes a ghost hunting group as a well based organization that is adhering to scientific methods of research more members will learn about the group and join, adding to the membership base. Prime locations that are reported to be haunted but have been off limits previously may become more accessible as a result of positive imaging provided by the media. Prestige of the group and professional attitudes will bring the group leads that they may investigate that may not otherwise have been made available.

Sometimes the media may alter your story and this may cause the group to be misunderstood. Some news agencies have reported on ghost hunters while playing the "Ghostbusters" theme song in the background and undermine the integrity of the group. Additionally, if the media is participating in an investigation they may taint the scene with their cameras, bright lights, microphones as they are more interested in getting an entertaining story than in conducting research. Sometimes to make a story more saleable to the station manager the reporter may gather their own data and come to their own conclusions, chop the organizations story into pieces and present a piece that is not what the ghost hunters had intended.

Still, the advantages of good public relations outweigh the disadvantages. TV, Radio and Newspaper are always looking for a good story. Use a press release to keep them informed of your group and what they are attempting to accomplish. A one page format you may want to us is provided here:

Press Release from Ghost Hunters Group

To: Who the release is sent to, local newspapers, television and media sources
Title: A catchy title to get the editors attention
Contact Information – Name and number of the person releasing the information
Date of the press release: Date release is sent out

Topic Line: Specific information about the upcoming event. Include who, what, when, where, why and how as well as why this is of interest to the media subscribers.

Information about the group: Information about the organization and group that the editor may be interested in for a follow up story.

Example of a Press Release Reviewing Movie
To: Local newspapers, television and media sources
Local Ghost Hunters to View White Noise Movie Release on
January 7, 2005
Contact Information – John Adams, President 253-208-1234
Release Date: December 30, 2004

The Amateur Ghost Hunting Organization of Seattle and Tacoma
(A.G.H.O.S.T.) will attend the opening of the movie "White Noise"
which details how EVP may be used to contact the dead. The
screening will take place at the Auburn- Cinema 17 Super Mall
Theater: (Interesting to note that the theater is reported to be haunted
as well -A spirit is reported to be found in the projection area.
Movies turn off by themselves in theaters 2, 9, and 17 for no
apparent reason.)
The group will attend the movie as a group of about 20 researchers
who will be available before and after the showing to answer
questions about ghost hunting or EVP. The volunteer organization
conducts ghost investigations in the Northwest and has a web site at
www.aghost.us.

About the Organization
The Amateur Ghost Hunting Organization of Seattle and Tacoma
(A.G.H.O.S.T.) is the most active ghost hunting group in the state of
Washington. This non-profit voluntary organization with over 100
members has open membership meetings twice a month in Federal
Way. The organization seeks serious and open-minded people who
would want to volunteer and help form an investigation team in the
northwest area.

Some investigations could involve over night stays in haunted
places and other activities. A.G.H.O.S.T. actively seeks individuals
who want to learn about the spirit world around us and the curious
are welcome to attend the open meetings. In order to participate in
ghost investigation members must be trained as an observer, a
technician or a psychic. Training is provided at no charge to
members.

211

There are three types of participants in a ghost hunt. Observers must be open minded, yet understand how the human mind can be tricked into seeing things that are natural occurrences and attribute them to ghostly phenomenon. The technicians use scientific instruments such as meters and gauges to seek out the true anomaly by eliminating natural and man made anomalies. Psychics use their sixth sense to explain what is happening in the area. All three types of members must agree that something unexplained happened at a particular time and place for the ghost hunters to agree that they have found something substantial.

Example of a Press Release

Press Release Ghost Hunters Conference
To: Local newspapers, television and media sources
Ghost Hunters conference in Port Townsend
Release on August, 2005
Contact Information – Ross Allison, President (253) 253 203-4383
Release Date: September 1, 2005

The Amateur Ghost Hunting Of Seattle - Tacoma (A.G.H.O.S.T.) will host their third annual ghost hunters' conference at Fort Worden Castle in Port Townsend on November 12 and 12, 2005. This educational weekend is open to the public with lectures, speakers and classes on such topics as Electronic Voice Phenomenon, Ghost Hunting Equipment, Historical Haunting versus Urban Legends and more. Participants will have the opportunity to participate in ghost hunting expeditions on Fort Worden, Port Townsend and local cemeteries. Members of AGHOST have been trained to conduct ghost investigations and will share their knowledge and experiences with those who attend the conference. A vendor fair will be held on Saturday with books and ghost related material available for sale to the general public.

About the Organization AGHOST is the most active volunteer ghost hunting group in Northwest Washington that conducts ghost investigations throughout the country. They can be contacted through their web site at www.aghost.us. This non-profit voluntary organization has open membership meetings twice a month in Federal Way. Investigations involve over night stays in haunted places. A.G.H.O.S.T. actively seeks individuals who want to learn about the spirit world around us and the curious are welcome to attend the open meetings. In order to become a member people attend a new member's orientation. After joining the organization, members receive their Ghost Hunters handbook, name tag and membership card. In order to participate in ghost investigation members must be trained as an observer, a technician or a psychic. Training is provided at no charge to members. There are three types of participants in a ghost hunt. Observers must be open minded, yet understand how the human mind can be tricked into seeing things that are natural occurrences and attribute them to ghostly phenomenon. The technicians use scientific instruments such as meters and gauges to seek out the true anomaly by eliminating natural and man made anomalies. Psychics use their sixth sense to explain what is happening in the area. All three types of members must agree that something unexplained happened at a particular time and place for the ghost hunters to agree that they have found something substantial.

AMATEUR GHOST HUNTERS OF SEATTLE, TACOMA

AGHOST BY-LAWS

ARTICLE I

Name and Jurisdiction

1. This Organization shall be known as AGHOST, Amateur Ghost Hunters of Seattle Tacoma, and has been in existence under that name since October 31, 2001.
2. The jurisdiction of this organization is worldwide with a special emphasis on the Northwest United States.
3. The principal office of this organization shall be located in the State of Washington. The organization may have such other branches either inside or outside the State of Washington as the Executive Officers may require from time to time.

ARTICLE II

Objectives

1. The Organization is a paranormal research organization. The objectives of this Organization shall be:
   a. To scientifically and without prejudice explore the realm of the supernatural with a special emphasis on the topics of ghosts, hauntings, poltergeists and life after death
   b. To explore the paranormal through on-site investigations at alleged haunted locations with the aid of technical equipment and psychic investigators
   c. Conduct investigations in homes and/or businesses at no charge
   d. All members of each investigation team will be thoroughly trained in their areas of responsibility and will continue receiving updated training as needed
   e. To gather all forms of evidence including, but not limited to: psychic impressions, photographs, video, audio, any physical proof and validation through research of historical data.

f. To report such findings in the Organization's message board and website as well as other media venues.

g. Maintain confidentiality as required

2. To receive, manage, invest, expend or otherwise use the funds and property of this Organization to carry out the duties and to achieve the objectives set forth in these By-Laws and for such additional purposes and objects consistent with the interests of this Organization and its members, directly or indirectly.

ARTICLE III

Officers

1. **Number of Officers.** The Organization shall be governed seven officers, consisting of a President, Vice President, Secretary, Technical director, Observer Director, Psychic Director and an Officer at large.

2. **Election.** The seven (7) Officers shall be elected to take office for such terms as provided in Section 5 below. The elections shall be carried out in accordance with Articles V and VI.

3. **Vacancies.** In the event a vacancy occurs for any reason, a Member shall be elected by a majority vote of the remaining Officers, whether or not the remaining Officers constitute a quorum, to fill such vacancy(s) for the remainder of the unexpired term(s). In the event a vacancy occurs in the position of President, the Vice-President shall fill the President's unexpired term. The position of Vice-President will then be filled by special election and will be elected by a majority vote of the general membership to fill the unexpired term. If the position of Treasurer or Secretary becomes vacant, a special election will be held and a member will be elected by a majority vote of the general membership to fill such vacancy for the remainder of the term.

4. **Dates of Tenure.** Tenure of office shall be from the end of the annual general meeting of the Organization until and including the following year's annual general meeting. The calendar year shall be the fiscal year of Organization.

5. **Terms.** The Officers elected by the membership as provided in Sections 1 and 2 above shall serve terms of two (2) years.

6. **Meetings.** The Officers shall have regular meetings at such time and at such places as it shall by resolution determine. Special meetings may be called by the President or by a majority of the members of the Officers.

7. **Quorum.** A majority of the seven Officers shall constitute a quorum for the transaction of business.

8. **Voting.** A quorum being present, decisions shall (with exceptions noted herein) be carried by an affirmative majority.

9. **Informal Action.** Action taken by the Officers without a meeting is nevertheless considered action if written consent to the action in question is signed by all the Officers and filed with minutes of the proceedings, whether done before or after the action so taken.

10. **Records.** Outgoing Officers are responsible for turning over to their successors all records, money, and other items associated with their offices which are the property of the Organization in proper condition and within one (1) week of the termination of their office.

11. **Removal.** A member of the Officers may be removed from office by the President if he/she fails to fulfill his/her delegated duties.

ARTICLE IV

Officers

1. PRESIDENT SHALL:

- preside over the regular, annual, and special meetings of the organization
- serve as the chief public relations officer
- promote agenda of the Organization
- take appropriate steps to maintain existing members and enroll new members.
- develop protocol for new members' meetings
- coordinate new members meetings
- chair committee for handbook development
- provide to the Officers for approval the new members' meeting protocol and handbook
- request research and coordinate research efforts with the Research Director
- in the absence of the Vice-President/Treasurer, sign contracts on behalf of the Organization
- shall bring to the Officers any and all concerns of the membership
- provide input into agendas for regular, Officers and special meetings
- perform such other duties as may be prescribed by the By-laws and as may properly be required by vote of the Officers

2. VICE-PRESIDENT SHALL:
- assist the President in the performance of his duties
- serve as acting President in the absence of the President
- assist and counsel with the President
- be responsible for the publicity of the Organization's meetings and activities, act as Client Coordinator who:
  - o shall coordinate all walk-throughs and assign a walk-through number
  - o shall coordinate all investigations and assign an investigation number
- request research and coordinate research efforts with the Research Director
- shall bring to the Officers any and all concerns of the membership

- provide input into agendas for regular, Officers and special meetings
- perform such other duties as may be prescribed by the By-laws and as may properly be required by vote of the Officers

3. SECRETARY SHALL:

- prepare the agenda for all general meetings
- record the minutes of all general meetings
- prepare the annual report for distribution to the general membership in a newsletter issued after the end of the program year
- notify the Officers of general meetings
- bring to the attention of the Board such matters as are required by the By-Laws
- be responsible for all correspondence of the Organization at the direction of the Officers
- maintain membership lists and files
- maintain files of all walk-throughs, investigations and expeditions
- print badges as required
- record attendance at all general meetings,
- oversee the production of client packages, which includes but not limited to, writing reports, compiling best photos, printing certificates
- maintain and keep confidential all documents as required
- perform such other duties as may be prescribed by the By-laws and as may properly be required by vote of the Officers
- Maintain Historical Documents

4. OFFICER AT-LARGE

- is (are) regular member(s) having voting power
- shall bring to the Officers any and all concerns of the membership
- provide input into agendas for meetings

5. OBSERVER DIRECTOR SHALL:

- develop and define the observer protocol, procedures and tests
- provide to the Officersl for approval all protocol, procedures and tests
- when possible, provide training (job shadowing) during expeditions, walk-throughs and investigations
- shall represent the interests of all observers to the Officers
- shall bring to the Officers any and all concerns of the membership
- provide input into agendas for meetings
- perform such other duties as may be prescribed by the By-laws and as may properly be required

- Observer director shall post upcoming walk-throughs, investigations and expeditions on the message board and may appoint a Calendar Coordinator to assist

6. PSYCHIC DIRECTOR SHALL:

- develop and define the psychic protocol, procedures and tests
- provide to the Officers for approval all protocol, procedures and tests
- when possible, provide training (job shadowing) during expeditions, walk-throughs and investigations
- shall represent the interests of all psychics to the Officers
- shall bring to the Officers any and all concerns of the membership
- provide input into agendas for regular, Officers and special meetings
- perform such other duties as may be prescribed by the By-laws and as may properly be required

7. TECHNOLOGY DIRECTOR SHALL:

- develop and define the tech protocol
- develop tests for members to pass to become a certified tech for the Organization
- create and define training and operational procedures for equipment (new and old)
- provide hands-on training for new members and additional training on new equipment and procedures for current techs as required
- provide tech training (job shadowing) during expeditions, walk-throughs and investigations
- certify members to use each piece of equipment
- maintain, repair, inspect and verify that all equipment is working correctly
- recommend equipment inventory for each category (Basic, Intermediate and Advanced)
- develop a recommended list of equipment
- research new devices which could assist the Organization in its investigations
- make recommendations to the Officers on Organization equipment purchases
- investigate new technology and trends in the paranormal fields
- make self available for all high profile cases or if media will be present
- ensure that a tech is available for all walk-throughs and investigations
- ensure that all lead techs are properly trained to lead and train future techs
- develop technical paranormal experiments
- provide to the Officers for approval all protocol, procedures and tests
- shall represent the interests of all techs to the Officers
- shall bring to the Officers any and all concerns of the membership
- provide input into agendas for regular, Officers and special meetings
- perform such other duties as may be prescribed by the By-laws and as may properly be required by vote of the Officers

OTHER POSITIONS

TREASURER SHALL:

- be responsible for all financial dealings of the Organization
- have charge of the financial accounts of the Organization
- chair all fundraising committees
- sign all contracts on behalf of the Organization. In the absence of the Vice-President/Treasurer, the President shall have the authority to sign contracts.
- collect dues and other debts on behalf of the Organization
- keep a complete record of all money received
- make necessary disbursements
- sign or authorize signature of such checks or other drafts upon the funds of the Organization as may be necessary
- keep a complete record of all money paid
- maintain accurate financial records
- prepare the annual financial report for distribution to the membership as part of the annual report.
- at all reasonable times, exhibit the books and accounts to any member of the Organization
- shall bring to the Officers any and all concerns of the membership
- perform such other duties as may be prescribed by the By-laws and as may properly be required

8. RESEARCH DIRECTOR SHALL:

- research known haunted, or reportedly haunted, locations, ghost stories and figures, either historical or present
- presenting results of findings either to the group as part of an investigation, group education i.e. classes, lectures, field trips or for inclusion in a final report
- research is done on a case by case basis as needed or as assigned by the President or Vice-President
- conduct research in person through interviews before a planned investigation (walkthroughs) if investigation is dealing with a historical location or figure
- conduct research through searching of records, documents etc. either by computer or in person at location where records are held.
- researching and answering requests for information from group members either in person or other medium such as electronic mail
- write for publication either to the public at large (newspaper, television or other media) or for internal use in field guides, trip guides and/or information for the Organization website
- will submit to the Officers for approval all material prior to dissemination in any form
- develop and define research protocol, procedures and tests
- provide to the Officers for approval all protocol, procedures and tests

- train research directors
- shall represent the interests of all researchers to the Officers
- shall bring to the Officers any and all concerns of the membership
- requirements (background in):
    - research
    - comprehension of history
    - public speaking
    - presentation
    - creative writing of at least one year or more is essential to this office, but should not be considered mandatory
- provide input into agendas for regular, Officers and special meetings
- perform such other duties as may be prescribed by the By-laws and as may properly be required

9. EXPEDITIONS DIRECTOR SHALL:

- develop and define the expedition protocol and procedures
- provide to the officers for approval all protocol, procedures and tests
- train expedition directors
- represent the interests of all expeditions directors to the Officers
- shall bring to the Officers any and all concerns of the membership
- provide input into agendas
- perform such other duties as may be prescribed by the By-laws and as may properly be required

10. TRAVEL AND EVENTS DIRECTOR SHALL:

- be dedicated and committed to coordinate quality events and travel for the purposes of research, education and investigation of ghostly phenomenon at the best value for members and guests
- keep costs low for all events while maintaining an outstanding level of quality
- work with the Officers to establish a schedule of events and travel for the upcoming year
- coordinate events which include, but not limited to:
    - Conferences
    - Special events
    - Overnight trips
    - Extended trips
- NOTE: Does not include Expeditions or Investigations which are the responsibility of other Officers members
- provide travel information packets to all members participating in each event as required
- provide release forms to participating members, collect signed forms and forward to the Secretary for filing

- shall bring to the Officers any and all concerns of the membership
- provide input into agendas for regular, Officers and special meetings
- perform such other duties as may be prescribed by the By-laws and as may properly be required by vote of the Officers

11. WEBMASTER SHALL:

- be appointed by the Officers
- maintain any web sites and e-mail discussion lists
- running error checks periodically to make sure website is functioning properly
- not be responsible for the content of the website
- bring to the Officers for approval all content prior to posting
- under the direction of the Officers:
  - be responsible for updating and maintaining the public and private areas of the website
  - updating specific sections with new information (photos, reports, etc.)
  - managing interactive areas of the private and public website (message boards, etc.)
- transferring or forwarding domain names
- keeping hosting account information updated
- informing president/vice president of upcoming hosting/domain payments
- shall bring to the Officers any and all concerns of the membership
- perform such other duties as may be prescribed by the By-laws and as may properly be required by vote of the Officers

ARTICLE V

Nominations and Elections

1. **Availability.** Any Member not willing or able to stand for nomination to the Officers and/or as President, Vice-President/Treasurer or Secretary for the next election must give notification of that fact in writing to the Chairman of the Election Committee. Members will be informed regarding the unavailable persons.
2. **Nomination.** The Election Committee shall issue a call by mail to all Members inviting them to nominate candidates for the Officers and for officer positions of President, Vice-President/Treasurer and Secretary from Members of the Organization. Attached to the call for nominations shall be a list of all members and of the Officers Members and Officers for the current year, with an indication of those officers whose terms of office are expiring and of those Members who have indicated a desire not to serve on the Officers and/or as

any officer. Nominations will be held at the next general meeting after the nomination announcement.

3. **Election.** The President, Vice-President/Treasurer, Secretary and Officers Members shall be elected every two (2) years by the general membership beginning in 2005. Voting shall be at the general meeting following the nomination general meeting. Voting shall be done by printed ballot at the general membership. No absentee ballots will be accepted or counted. A majority shall carry a vote.

4. **Voting.** A quorum being present, a majority shall carry a vote in any of the committees of the Organization.

5. **Ties.** Tie votes in the nominations and elections referred to in this section shall be decided by the tied nominees by using the Paper, Rock, Scissors method.

ARTICLE VII

Membership

1. **Member.** A member shall be a person in good standing and with fully paid membership dues.

2. **Honorary Member.** An Honorary Member shall be a person:
   a. who, in the opinion of the Officers, has made outstanding contributions to the advancement of the paranormal
   b. who has been nominated by three Officers Members
   c. who has been elected by a unanimous vote of the Officers. An Honorary Member shall not pay membership dues nor have voting rights in the Organization.

3. **Charter Members.** Anyone who was a Charter Member under the Organization at the time of its inception shall become a Charter Member of AGHOST.

Eligibility for Membership

1. Subject only to the specific conditions stated hereinafter, any person who has an interest in the paranormal shall be eligible for membership.
2. Applicants for membership must meet the following requirements:
   a. All Members must be at least eighteen (18) years of age and have a valid ID or driver's license prior to joining.
   b. He/she must fill out and sign a Membership Information Sheet.
   c. He/she must sign a Membership Agreement.
   d. He/she must attend a New Members Orientation.
3. Active Membership can be permanently revoked if:
   a. He/she refuses, or fails, to follow established By-Laws, protocols, policies or rules of the Organization.
   b. He/she advocates race, religious, sexual orientation or class hatred.
   c. He/she divulges privileged or confidential information to anyone outside the Organization.
   d. He/she attempts to undermine the credibility of the Organization in anyway.
   e. He/she violates any portion of the By-Laws, protocols, policies or rules of the Organization or membership agreement.
   f. No portion of membership dues will be reimbursed upon membership revocation.
4. Other membership points:
   a. The Organization has the exclusive right to deny membership to anyone who does not meet the standards set forth by the Organization.
   b. The Organization is not obligated in anyway to retain any individual not meeting the above mentioned criteria and/or any other criteria as deemed necessary by the Organization.

ARTICLE IX

Dues

1. **Notice.** Dues for members are to be paid annually. Notice of the dues for the ensuing year shall be mailed to the members as early as possible.
2. **Non-Payment.** Non-payment of dues within three (3) months of issuance of the notice shall result in termination from the Organization.
3. **Amounts.** Dues for members shall be set by the Officers from time to time. The Officers may also establish reductions in dues for designated subgroups (e.g., students, retired persons) or may set charges for late payment of dues as deemed necessary.
4. **Waiver.** In exceptional cases it shall be within the powers of the Officers by unanimous vote to authorize payment of dues of members from the Treasury of the Organization.

ARTICLE X

Meetings, Conference and Publications

1. **Meetings**
   a. General Meetings
      1) The Officers shall determine the dates, times and locations of regular meetings and shall provide for such meetings by resolution.
   b. Annual Meetings
      1) Annual meetings of the members shall be held in conjunction with the Annual Convention or at such other places and times as the Officers shall provide by resolution.
   c. Special Meetings
      1) Special meetings may be called by the President or by a majority of the members of the Officers.
2. **Conference**
   a. The Organization each year shall sponsor a Conference to promote the purposes and goals of the Organization.
   b. The Officers may from time to time sponsor other such meetings to further the educational and scientific goals of the Organization.
3. **Publication.** The Officers shall, by majority vote, elect an Editor or Editors for an indefinite term of office that shall be responsible for bringing out the Organization's publication(s) with the advice and consent of the Officers.
4. **Additional Publications.** Other publications may be issued at the discretion of the Officers.

Article XI

Official Logos

All logos of the Organization are copyrighted and remain the property of the Organization. These designs and logos cannot be reproduced without expressed written consent from the Officers.

ARTICLE XI

Rules of Procedure

All meetings of the Organization shall be held in accordance with Robert's Rules of Order, Revised.

ARTICLE XII

Amendments

Amendments to the by-laws may be proposed by any Member and submitted to the Secretary. The latter shall prepare copies of the proposed amendment and submit it to all Officers Members. An amendment shall become effective if approved by a two-thirds majority of the total number of Officers Members.

Glossary

Apparition: An unexpected or preternatural appearance; a ghost; a specter; a phantom. A rare photographic anomaly normally captured on film. An apparition is a ghost that has taken human form.

Aura: A luminous radiation often reported around beings usually observed with special equipment or by a person with enhanced psychic ability.

Discarnate: Having no material body or form

Dream communication: A method of communicating with the dead by interpreting dreams.

Ectoplasm: The substance supposed to emanate from the body of the medium during a trance. Usually resembles smoke or fog in photographs.

Electromagnetic Field: The field of force associated with electric charge in motion, having both electric and magnetic components and containing a definite amount of electromagnetic energy; believed to be generated when spirits manifest.

EMF Detector: An instrument for measuring the magnitude and direction of a magnetic field. Also known as a Gauss Meter or magnetometer.

Electronic Voice Phenomenon (EVP) A phenomenon where voices or images are captured on a recording medium, usually a tape recorder. Often no sound is heard while the tape is recording but on playback distinct voices may be heard.

Epicenter: The region that seems to be in the center of activity being investigated such as the focal area of ghostly activity.

Extra Sensory: Residing beyond or outside the normal senses.

ESP: Extra Sensory Perception The ability to perceive things outside the normal range of senses.

Ghost: A disembodied soul; especially, the soul of a dead person believed to be an inhabitant of the unseen world or to appear to the living in bodily likeness. The spirit of a dead person, especially one believed to appear in bodily likeness to living persons or to haunt former habitats. Soul, Spirit, Demon. The disembodied spirit of a dead person, conceived of an appearing to the living as a pale, shadowy apparition.

Ghost Hunt: going to a place were there have been no sightings of ghosts and trying to catch some on film (video and photos), sounds, eyewitness, etc. (graveyards are the number one place to start, churches, schools and older buildings too).

Ghost Investigation: The act of going to a known haunted place and recording data (video, photos, audio, and temperatures), notes, interviews and other evidence to prove/disprove the haunting. To assist the owners and the spirits in moving on and leaving the place if they want that. The assistance can be either directly assisting the owner with the situation or putting them in contact with experienced groups or individuals that will try to resolve the situation. Assistance can be something as simple as educating them and providing options.

Haunt(ing/ed): A place, area, or building that exhibits ghostly apparitions or other signs of ghostly activity. Inhabited by, or subject to the visits of, apparitions; frequented by a ghost. Haunt: Visit often or continually. Frequented by ghosts.

Hoax: An act taken in an attempt to trick or dupe people or ghost hunters into believing that a place is haunted when there is no ghostly activity taking place.

Manifestation: One of the forms in which someone or something, such as a divine being, is revealed; the materialized form of a spirit.

Medium: A person thought to have the power to communicate with the spirits of the dead or with agents of another world or dimension. Also called psychic.

Mist: A photographed anomaly that appears as a wall of light that is not seen at the time of the photograph; believed to be the appearance of a ghost or spirit of the dead.

Orb: Glowing balls of light or energy that often accompany a haunting and show up on photographs. A photographed anomaly that appears as a ball of light and may occasionally seem to be moving that is not seen at the time of the photograph; believed to represents a ghost.

Ouija Board: A trademark used for a board with the alphabet and other symbols on it, and a planchette that is thought, when touched with the fingers, to move in such a way as to spell out spiritualistic and telepathic messages on the board.

Paranormal: Literally, beyond normal. An event or instance which cannot be explained using our natural or normal science or rationale.

Percipient: Capable of perception; one who perceives

Possession: Domination by an evil spirit

Psychic: A person apparently sensitive to non physical forces. Also referred to as a medium.

Paranormal: Beyond the range of normal experience or scientific explanation.

Parapsychology: The study of the evidence for psychological phenomena, such as telepathy, clairvoyance, and psycho kinesis, that is inexplicable by science.

Phantom: Something apparently seen, heard, or sensed, but having no physical reality; a ghost or an apparition. Something that seems to appear to the sight but has no physical existence; Apparition, Vision, Specter. Something to be feared or dreaded.

Poltergeist: A ghost that manifests itself by noises, rappings, and the creation of disorder. Responsible for mysterious noisy disturbances, moving or misplacing of objects. Some poltergeists have been reported to cause physical harm to people.

Portal: A doorway to another dimension through which spirits, ghosts and other entities may be able to pass.

Séance: A meeting normally conducted by a medium in an effort to receive spirit communications.

Shadow People: Unexplained shadows that appear in photographs and video, believed to be associated with evil or angry spirits or possessing negative energy. Some observers have reported seeing them with their naked eyes.

Spirit: An entity which has a consciousness and is able to interact with investigators that haunts an area

Supernatural: Not existing in nature or subject to explanation according to natural laws; not physical or material.

Vortex: A photographed anomaly that appears as a funnel or rope-like image that is not seen at the time of the photograph; believed to represents a 'ghost'.

Wraith: Guardian; a ghost. Spectral figure of a person supposedly seen as a premonition just before that person dies.

Units of Measurement - electrical

tesla (T) – The SI unit of *magnetic flux density* (the magnetic field). The *tesla* is equivalent to 1 *weber* per square meter.

weber (Wb) – The SI unit of *magnetic flux*, which is defined as the strength and the extent of the magnetic field.

volt (V) – The SI unit of *electric potential.*

maxwell (Mx) – Unit of *magnetic flux*. The *maxwell* is equivalent to 10^{-8} *weber*, or 1 *gauss* per square centimeter.

gauss (G) – Unit of *magnetic flux density*. The *gauss* is equivalent to 10^{-4} *tesla* (1 gauss = 1 microtesla).

Units of Measurement - radiological

Curie (Ci) – The unit that described radioactivity, in terms of the number of decays per second. Specifically defined as 3.7×10^{10} decays per second. This unit has been replaced by the SI derived unit, the *becquerel.*

Becquerel (Bq) – The SI derived unit of radioactivity. This unit measures the activity of a sample of material in which one nucleus decays per second.

Roentgen (R) – A unit of radiation exposure equal to the quantity of ionizing radiation that will produce one electrostatic unit of electricity in one cubic centimeter of dry air at 0°C and standard atmospheric pressure.

REM (*Roentgen Equivalent Man*) – This unit is used to describe the *equivalent dose* or *effective* dose of ionizing radiation. Specifically, one **rem** is the amount of ionizing radiation required to produce the same <u>effect</u> as one *rad* of high-energy x-rays. The **rem** unit is derived from the *rad*, but is obtained by multiplying by what is called a *quality factor* to determine the biological effect of the adsorbed dose. This unit is still often encountered, but is considered obsolete and replaced by the SI derived unit, the *sievert*.

Sievert (Sv) – The SI derived unit which is equal to 100 rems exactly.

RAD (*Radiation Absorbed Dose*) – A unit of energy absorbed from ionizing radiation. Different materials when exposed to the same amount of radiation will absorb different amounts of energy. A **rad** measures the actual amount of energy that is transferred to the mass. Typically this unit is adjusted for the absorption rate of a biological mass (such as a human). This unit is still often encountered, but is considered obsolete and replaced by the SI derived unit, the *gray*.

Gray (Gy) – The SI derived unit equivalent to 100 *rads*.

About the Authors

Joe Teeples has over 25 years as a professional investigator. He has investigated paranormal activity around the world. Such unexplained phenomenon as Bigfoot, Yeti, UFO's, ESP, Ghosts and hauntings have been researched using his scientific methods. Mr. Teeples holds an MBA from the University of Wisconsin.

Ross Allison
Ross is the founding President of AGHOST, the largest, most active ghost hunting group in the Northwest using scientific methods to study ghosts. His interest began with ghost stories told by his mother, and his fifteen years of experience pursuing the unknown has lead him to the organization of the Seattle based ghost hunting group.
The organization has hosted training sessions, expeditions and investigations into the paranormal for five years. Ross is well versed in the study of the paranormal, and conducts classes at the college level on such topics as Ghostology and Psychic Development. He can be found giving lectures around the country on ghosts and the paranormal. Mr. Allison has been on television, radio and in the press on a routine basis concerning ghost hunting.

Made in the USA
San Bernardino, CA
06 December 2012